STARS!

A Study of 19th Century Star Quilts
By the American Quilt Study Group

STARS!

A Study of 19th Century Star Quilts By The American Quilt Study Group

Editor: Deb Rowden
Designer: Kelly Ludwig
Photography: Aaron T. Leimkuehler
Illustration: Eric Sears
Technical Editor: Kathe Dougherty
Production assistance: Jo Ann Groves

Published by:
Kansas City Star Books
1729 Grand Blvd.
Kansas City, Missouri, USA 64108
All rights reserved
Copyright © 2011 The Kansas City Star Co.

First edition, first printing

ISBN: 978-1-61169-003-3

Library of Congress Control Number: 2010943392

Printed in the United States of America by Walsworth Publishing Co., Marceline, MO

To order copies, call StarInfo at

(816) 234-4636 and say "Books."

The Quilter's Home Page

www.PickleDish.com

DEDICATION

To the past and present board members of the American Quilt Study Group for their dedication and service that has helped the organization to flourish.

ACKNOWLEDGEMENTS

On behalf of the Board of Directors of the American Quilt Study Group, I wish to thank all those individuals who made this book possible.

- All of the AQSG members who created the stunning quilts that are presented in this volume.

- The owners of the inspiration quilts who granted permission for them to be studied and to be shown in this book.

- Greta Van Den Berg-Nestle and Georgia Chiorella, Chair and Assistant Chair of the Biennial Quilt Study, whose creativity and countless hours of work brought this book to fruition.

- Laurel Horton for her introduction and for her years of dedicated service to AQSG.

- Bobbi Finley and Penny Tucker, who created the Quilt Study Project in 2000 and directed four of the first five Studies, and Connie Nordstrom, who directed the third Quilt Study.

- Jane Miller, Judy Schwender, Carol Jones, Bettina Havig and Deb Rowden for patterning skills.

- Deb Rowden for her organizational and editing skills.

- Kelly Ludwig for putting together a beautiful book of our quilts.

- The exhibition sites for the Quilt Study Traveling Exhibit and the donors who have made the traveling exhibit possible.

- Judy J. Brott Buss, Executive Director, and Anne E. Schuff, Member Services Coordinator of AQSG, for all they do for the organization.

Mary G. Persyn
AQSG President

CONTENTS

INTRODUCTION

This is a book of Star quilts, 19th Century Stars to be exact. They were created for the 2010 Quilt Study project by members of the American Quilt Study Group, knowledgeable people who are passionate about quilts, their past, present and future.

Thirty-nine quilts were created – 25 of them are travelling the country to selected venues into the year 2012. Each quilt is shown, along with a statement by the quiltmaker sharing what she learned as she created her Study Quilt. When possible, we've included a photograph of the quilt that inspired the project.

Patterns for 10 of the quilts are included, starting on page 61. You'll also find information about the process of quilt study, past AQSG Studies, and exhibit venues for these quilts.

Through hard work and tenacity, AQSG has become the leader in quilt scholarship; AQSG was founded in 1980 by a group who believed that quilts hold unique stories and essential history that has long been overlooked, or in some cases lost altogether. They created an organization that encourages a sound academic approach to quilt research and history, and that provides opportunities for quilt historians and others to share their discoveries. Learn more about AQSG on page 112.

Enjoy!

THE AQSG QUILT STUDY: THE LEARNING OF PROCESS AND THE PROCESS OF LEARNING

By Laurel Horton

As a group, quiltmakers share a body of traditions, attitudes, and terminology that provide a sense of community and continuity. Within this common sphere, however, individual quiltmakers express themselves through an astonishing variety of motivations, techniques, and skill levels. Every quilt is the result of a unique process of design and construction; and the trajectory of a particular quilt is individualized by the convergence of specific influences, both internal and external, at the time of its creation.

Quilt research includes studies of both historic and contemporary subjects, and the annual volumes of *Uncoverings* (the journal of AQSG) have included a number of pioneering explorations into the quiltmaking process. For the inaugural 1980 volume, Lucy Hilty wrote "A Passion for Quiltmaking," based on her own experience and the results of a survey conducted by Marilyn Davis, a quilt shop owner[1]. An unidentified quiltmaker shared these thoughts in response to the survey:

Quiltmaking is the emotional center of my life. The planning is my most creative outlet, and the piecing and quilting my meditation. ...There are certain tasks (marking) which seem tedious, and others, equally as routine and demanding precision (piecing) which seem glorious. ...There is, in the process, in its life, ... the evolution of a relationship with the work. ...When I began to make quilts I felt as if a central part of me had come home.

The emotional state described here is familiar to many quiltmakers and other creative individuals, who experience the creative process as a coming together of their mental, emotional, and physical facilities to produce a state of heightened awareness in the present moment. Others describe the emergence of an impression of wholeness, satisfaction, or purpose. Not everyone who makes a quilt is touched deeply, but those who find fulfillment in the process generally want to do it again.

The idea of a "quilt study" originated among members of AQSG who wished to use the quiltmaking process as a way of learning. By selecting a particular historic quilt as inspiration, this study offers an opportunity for a "two-way" exploration. First, observation or replication of a historic textile may bring insights into the way the original maker approached the process. A close examination may reveal, for example, that she pieced individual blocks by hand but added sashing and border by machine, suggesting that she constructed the small blocks as "pick-up work" at odd moments or while visiting; then sat at the machine to assemble the finished blocks into a much less portable quilt top.

Second, deciding how to interpret the historic piece offers a window on one's own attitudes, assumptions, preferences, and limitations. I might observe the frustration and tension that emerge with my first clumsy attempts to piece hexagon patchwork over paper templates. If I persevere, I may perceive the release and relief as my fingers learn the choreography and the process becomes more graceful and satisfying. Working through obstacles or experimenting to find solutions rewards risk-taking behavior, or, at worst, successfully identifies methods that do not work.

The participants in AQSG's 2010 Quilt Study each selected an "inspiration" piece, often described as one that "spoke" to them in some way. As a museum volunteer, Nancy Losee spent 13 months helping to conserve the quilt that she chose for her study. The process of stabilizing delicate fabrics and seams provided an opportunity for an intimate, tactile relationship with the piece. Cindy Hamilton selected a quilt from her own collection, a faded, tattered textile purchased in an antique store. She decided to created a replica in order to "save the unusual pattern from extinction." Beverly Birkmire was one of several participants who were inspired by the image of a striking quilt on a book cover.

Having selected their inspiration pieces, participants had to determine how to translate the design in a smaller format. Julia Zgliniec chose a star made from one-inch diamonds. Instead of reducing the size of the pieces, she drafted a design using fewer diamonds that would "recreate the overall feel of the original." Many participants aimed for a close replication of the original fabrics, making use of the many lines of reproduction 19th century fabrics currently available. For a more contemporary approach, Donna Starley chose bright yellow and hot pink batiks to mimic the colors in the original quilt and to "add a little charm." June Ross sought out reproduction chintz to replicate the original quilt as best she could, then added beads "for a little sparkle."

Knowing something about the maker of the inspiration quilt can add a further dimension to the study process. Starting with the name of the maker, Carolyn Maruggi identified a likely candidate through genealogical research. The highlight of Marti Phelps's study of a museum quilt came with a conversation with the donor, the 87-year-old great-granddaughter of the maker. Even "orphan" quilts—those of unknown provenance—offer puzzles to ponder. Marjorie Farquharson wondered, while examining her inspiration piece, whether a later quilter added the simple patchwork blocks around the more complex center star, or if this was the maker's original intention.

Dale Drake found that the maker of her inspiration quilt was "meticulous in her attention to detail," and she tried to imitate this approach in her own hand-piecing and hand-quilting. Curious about the home-produced fibers and fabrics in her chosen piece, Greta VanDenBerg-Nestle bought a spinning wheel and learned to spin the wool yarn. She then wove the fabrics for the top and back. At the other end of the technological spectrum, Sally Ambrose used computer software to scale down her pattern, then pieced and quilted by machine. Despite these tools, she found the process difficult: "All those set-in seams nearly defeated me. I constructed, deconstructed, and reconstructed until the stars were as square as I could manage. Determination carried me onward to completion."

The completion of the process, of course, results in the "birth" of a quilt, which then takes on a life of its own. Carol Godreau and Maureen Gregoire were inspired by a museum-owned quilt, and the director is delighted with the result: "We love this quilt. By reproducing the quilt for the AQSG Study, more people will see what a truly wonderful quilt it is."

The finished piece is also the material record of the maker's experience, suffused with a mélange of intangible associations, memories, and questions. Sandra Starley pondered the changes in technology over time: "It is always enlightening to see how another quilter addressed the same challenges and what they accomplished without rotary cutters and all the other gadgets we 'must have.'" The participants in the AQSG Quilt Study took the opportunity to stretch themselves, to experiment, and to work through personal, as well as technical, challenges. Confessing "a general aversion to appliqué," Xenia Cord was intrigued by the methods used in an unusual appliqué quilt. With her sense of humor still intact, she reflected on the process, "Working out the appliqué was a minefield. I hated making this little piece, but I'm glad I did it."

ABOUT THE AUTHOR

Laurel Horton is an independent quilt researcher, author, and editor. A native of Kentucky, she holds a BS in English and a MS in library science from the University of Kentucky, and a MS in folklore from UNC-Chapel Hill. Horton wrote the 2005 award-winning book, *Mary Black's Family Quilts: Memory and Meaning in Everyday Life*. A member of AQSG since 1982, she is a former board member, past president, and editor of *Uncoverings* from 1987-1993, and 2008-2012.

---

[1] Lucille Hilty, "A Passion for Quiltmaking," in Uncoverings 1980, ed. Sally Garoutte (Mill Valley, CA: American Quilt Study Group, 1981), 13-17. The following year, Marilyn Davis, who described herself as "a somewhat frustrated anthropologist who happens to own a fabric store," published an article summarizing the entire survey, documenting the demographics and behaviors of quiltmakers during the early years of the quilt revival of the late-twentieth century: Marilyn Davis, "The Contemporary American Quilter: A Portrait," in Uncoverings 1981, ed. Sally Garoutte (Mill Valley, CA: American Quilt Study Group, 1982), 45-51. Davis owned a quilt shop called Patience Corners, in Albany, CA.

AQSG Quilt Studies History

By Bobbi Finley

AQSG was born around Sally Garoutte's kitchen table. A somewhat similar story might be applied to the birth of the AQSG Quilt Studies.

In the spring of 2000, AQSG members Penelope Tucker and Terry Barnes gathered in Bobbi Finley's home in San Jose, California to welcome fellow member, Terry Clothier Thompson, who was in town teaching. Admiring a tall stack of reproduction fabrics and a recent book showcasing an exhibit of antique chintz quilts, the four talked of making quilts from the book with the fabrics.

The conversation evolved and it was decided to offer AQSG members the opportunity to study a chintz quilt from the period 1790 – 1860 by making a reproduction of the chosen quilt and to provide information regarding what they learned in the process. What fabrics were used, what construction methods and quilting styles? To ponder about the woman who made the original; who was she? What was her design inspiration? Why did she choose those fabrics? Why did she do "that"?

Bobbi volunteered to get Board approval and coordinate the exhibit. An invitation to join the Study appeared in the next AQSG newsletter, *Blanket Statements*. The quilts would be presented at our annual seminar in Lincoln, Nebraska. The local Seminar committee provided space to hang the 21 quilts of the 13 participants who joined the first Study.

At the next Seminar, participants of the 2000 Study met and decided to do it again! Penny Tucker stepped forward to coordinate the Study - the topic was early Crib Quilts. More than 50 quilts were exhibited at Seminar in 2002.

Connie Nordstrom coordinated the third Quilt Study, Two-Color quilts. Twenty-two participants exhibited quilts at Seminar in 2004 in Vancouver, Washington. The Quilt Study was beginning to be an important part of AQSG Seminar.

The topic of Pre-1840's Bed Coverings was chosen for the 2006 Study in Connecticut. At that point Bobbi and Penny stepped back in to coordinate the studies on an ongoing basis. The small exhibit space at Seminar that year was overflowing with 30 Study Quilts.

Mid-19th Century Red and Green Quilts were the 2008 Study in Ohio. By this time the Studies had become so popular that a cap was placed on the number of study quilts accepted due to limited exhibit space. Forty-eight quilts were exhibited at Seminar. For the first time, the quilts were juried to select a more manageable number of 25 quilts for the traveling exhibit.

Thanks to AQSG members, exhibits have toured to various venues, including many museums, creating interest in AQSG and the study of quilt history. In addition, study quilts have graced the pages of quilting magazines and books, creating even greater understanding of antique quilts. Many members have participated in all six studies.

Guidelines for the 2010 Quilt Study

AQSG invited members to create a reproduction quilt for the sixth biennial AQSG Quilt Study for the 2010 Seminar in Minneapolis, Minnesota. The focus of the 2010 study was 19th Century Star Quilts. Participation was encouraged as a way of learning about our quilt heritage and to promote AQSG.

Participants were asked to follow these guidelines:

- The quilt may contain one or 100 stars but it must read as a "star quilt".

- You may reproduce a portion of the original, or a scaled down version of any star quilt of the period. You may make an exact replica of the original quilt, but it is not required. You may also make a quilt that is "inspired" by the original.

- While many star patterns are pieced, your stars or other parts of the quilt may be appliquéd if the original quilt was appliquéd.

- Overall maximum measurement of 200" for all four sides will be strictly enforced.

- Each participant will be limited to submitting one quilt.

- Incomplete projects will not be accepted. All exhibited quilts must be finished (i.e., quilted and bound). All quilts must also have a standard sleeve attached, and a label with your name and address. An additional label with your entry number (when assigned) will also be required.

- To be considered a Quilt Study Participant, each participant must submit completed and signed release documents together with documentation of the inspiration for their project, including a photograph of the inspiration piece and a statement about the work, such as why the particular quilt was chosen for study and what was learned from study of the quilt. The statements should not exceed 200 words.

- Two release forms will be required. The first is to be signed by the owner of the original quilt or quilt image allowing the participant to reproduce the quilt (either in part or in total) and further allows use of images of the original quilt or quilt image as part of all exhibits and publications related to the quilt study. The second document is to be signed by the participant granting permission for AQSG to show the study quilts, and use images of the study quilts for publication, promotion, etc.

- The photograph that is required of the inspiration quilt must be in .jpg file format. If you do not have the capability of creating a .jpg file, this generally can be accomplished at any copy shop.

- Any quilt that does not fit within the guidelines of this study will not be considered for inclusion in the travelling exhibit.

- Only AQSG members may participate.

Traveling Exhibit Schedule

AQSG's 2010 Quilt Study of Star Quilts were received and displayed at AQSG's 31st Annual Seminar in Minneapolis in October, 2010. Following Seminar, 25 of the study quilts were selected to travel as a group to various venues for exhibition representing AQSG. Here's the schedule:

October 30 – November 7, 2010:

International Quilt Festival, Houston, Texas

January 3, 2011 - February 6, 2011:

Latimer Quilt and Textile Center, Tillamook, Ore.

February 25, 2011 - June 5, 2011:

Monroe County History Center, Bloomington, Ind.

July – August 2011:

New England Quilt Museum, Lowell, Mass.

September 17-18, 2011:

Faithful Circle Quilters Show, Woodridge, Ill.

November 2011 – January 2012:

Rocky Mountain Quilt Museum, Golden, Colo.

March 2012:

Dallas Quilt Celebration, Dallas, Texas

April – August 2012:

International Quilt Study Center & Museum, Lincoln, Neb.

More venues may be added, check the American Quilt Study Group website for updates:

http://www.americanquiltstudygroup.org/QS%20Exhibit%20Schedule.asp

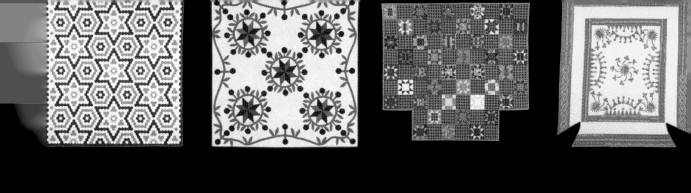

STARS!
STUDY QUILTS

BETHLEHEM STAR

Nancy L. Losee
Williamsburg, Virginia
36" x 36"

A Bethlehem Star quilt, 92" x 92", in the textile collection of Colonial Williamsburg, became my volunteer assignment for conservation in preparation for a star quilt exhibit at the DeWitt-Wallace Museum. Working on selected areas of this quilt for 13 months allowed me to study it extensively: fabrics, prints, values, color sequences and most of all the skill to create something of beauty that endures for years. Documentation indicates the quilt was probably made in Alexandria, Virginia 1850-1880. It has 2,212 pieces.

When AQSG announced the star quilt study, I was challenged. It took one month to draft the pattern and three months to lay fabrics from my stash in proper color sequence. Value is most important! After the original, conserved quilt was displayed under glass at the museum, I saw for the first time the entire quilt instead of the small areas that I had delicately conserved. How could I select only a portion of this lovely quilt to replicate when its beauty was its entirety? Thus my 36" x 36" replication of the entire original quilt is made of reproduction fabrics of the 1850-1880 era and quilted exactly as the original.

I learned that when I view a quilt, I have not seen it in the depth that its maker did. From a distance I learned color value and placement are most important. After spending 13 months in the conservation process of the original quilt and with my interest in history, I found my thoughts drifting back to the post Civil War era and the Virginia quilter's life. I gained an appreciation for the meticulous piecing, enormous hours involved, and the maker's devotion to her undertaking.

MATHEMATICAL STAR

Julia D. Zgliniec
Poway, California
40.5" x 40.5"

I have always loved the large mathematical stars of the second quarter of the 19th century, particularly those made in the Mid-Atlantic States. I have always admired the needlework skills of the women who chose to make them. An unusual 12 point star variation from my collection was the inspiration for my study quilt.

The original quilt measured a huge 107" x 107". The 1" diamonds creating the star points were composed of hundreds of early prints. I chose to use the same 1" sized diamonds but the scale of the original would have been almost impossible to duplicate. I chose instead to recreate the overall feel of the original.

After the challenges of drafting the design, fabric selection followed and was the most enjoyable part of the process. The central star was machine pieced using contemporary strip piecing techniques. I hand pieced the Eight Point Stars which measure 2 7/8". Not wishing to hand quilt through all the seam allowances as did the original maker; I chose to quilt by machine and used the same pattern as the original to accentuate the star.

After completing this quilt, I am even more in awe of the skill of the unknown maker who collected the huge variety of fabrics, drafted a diamond that created a star of such magnitude, and quilted the design to compliment that star.

LOUISE'S STARS

Nancy Ostman
Groton, New York
50" x 50"

While documenting quilts at The History Center in Ithaca, NY, our study team was surprised by a bright, cheerful quilt. It seemed modern. But, indeed it was old (1840-1857). The colors and fabrics made us curious.

The maker, Anna Marie Louise Le Pine Treman (1794-1857), lived as a girl on the Caribbean island of Saint Dominique with her French father, who disappeared during a general massacre. Disguised as an "orange" girl by family servants, she escaped on a merchant ship bound for New York. There, she was unable to find relatives. She ended up living with the ship captain's family. Later Louise was recognized at Alexander Hamilton's funeral and reunited with her grandmother and brother.

I supposed that Louise's early life in Saint Dominique led her to choose bright colors for her quilt, speculating that the sky was dominant in her life on the island and at sea. When making the study quilt, I mostly used the brightest reproduction fabrics I could find, attempting to be true to Louise's choices of colors. I wondered how Louise found those bright fabrics in the 1800s, and if my impression of color from the era was distorted. I wondered if the bright quilt she made while living in central New York State was a refuge from the area's gray winters, as mine became. In my design, I tried to capture Louise's liveliness, sense of a big moving sky, and use of as many stars as she did.

MENNONITE LONE STAR

Bobbi Finley
San Jose, California
49.5" x 49.5"

I was first attracted to this star quilt because I'm very fond of the lone star pattern and the way it radiates. Also, this quilt included appliqué blocks. The maker of the original quilt is unknown but she was believed to be from a Mennonite family in Souderton, PA. She was an accomplished quiltmaker and very creative in her designs. I would love to ask her how she came up with her designs. The green leafy branch blocks are very unusual. I don't remember ever seeing this pattern and was not able to identify it. The red blocks are also appealing and again, I was unable to identify a pattern name for this block though it is similar to Honeybee and Turkey Tracks. The sawtooth borders were the perfect finish.

I scaled down the original quilt (which measures 95" x 95") to 50" square and drafted my own patterns. I decided that when the quilt was scaled down, the outer border would be too small to show off any feather quilting so I eliminated that border and the second sawtooth edge.

Drafting and stitching the lone star proved to live up to the reputation of these star patterns as being difficult but I persevered through the "unsewing" and resewing to achieve a star that lays flat with straight lines. The rest was pure pleasure.

Mariner's Compass Variation, 1850. Original courtesy of the Dinsmore Homestead Foundation, Burlington, KY

INDIGO STAR OF DINSMORE

Diane D. Livezey
Edgewood, Kentucky
34.5" x 34.5"

When the AQSG quilt study topic for 2010 was announced, I knew that this was my opportunity to explore the origin and construction of a quilt in the collection of the Dinsmore Homestead in Boone County, Kentucky. I had both sketches and photos of the indigo and white star quilt dated c. 1875. Unfortunately, I've been unsuccessful in my attempts to source the maker of the quilt which was gifted to the Homestead with no documentation. The star block is particularly unique. I have not found another with this piece placement. A quilt from mid-1800 Iowa with a different placement of the small four-pointed half-sun was found in the Quilt Index of the Alliance for American Quilts.

Using a pattern painstakingly drafted by a friend, I constructed the block by hand which was a task requiring many hours and extreme precision. I chose to reproduce the sawtooth borders with the same deviation from symmetry as the original quilt. I cannot believe that someone who spent countless hours in pursuit of perfection in the construction of the blocks would not have pursued uniformity in the borders. Thus I believe she/he intended for both sawtooth borders to be asymmetrical, especially when the extensive feather quilting is extremely well done - indicating the original was created by a master quilter.

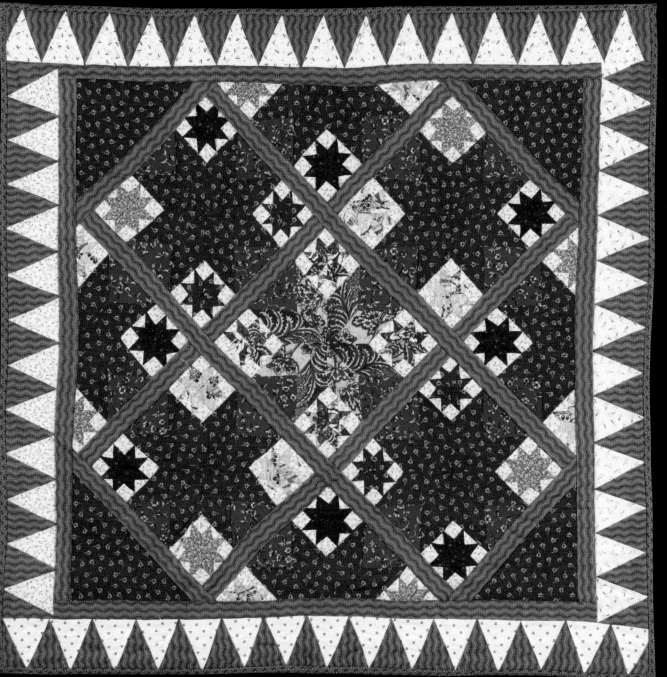

Courtesy of Cape Fear Museum, Wilmington, NC

CAPE FEAR STAR

Sally A. Ambrose
Leavenworth, Washington
33" x 33"

Permission to replicate the original quilt is courtesy of Cape Fear Museum, Wilmington, NC. Terri Hudgins, Registrar. No maker's name, no provenance from accession file.

The visual impact of this quilt caught me by surprise. I knew that I wanted this to be my study quilt. Would I be able to reduce the original 101 x 102.5" size to fit the parameters of the study challenge? Would I be able to find just the right reproduction fabrics?

I used Block Base #3735a templates for the 2 1/2" and 8" diamond blocks. Julia Zgliniec gave me the chintz-style fabric. The blue, green and red fabrics were purchased from Reproduction Fabric and the other fabrics were from my own stash. My husband cut 1/4" acrylic for the large templates, and the small diamond templates are cardstock covered with thin acrylic. It was constructed by machine and hand piecing and hand quilted.

All those set-in seams nearly defeated me. I constructed deconstructed and reconstructed until the stars were as square as I could manage. At one point, I gave serious consideration to turning the quilt into potholders. Determination carried me onward to completion.

To the amazing unknown quiltmaker - this is your quilt! Enjoy.

EAGLE MEDALLION

Carol Godreau & Maureen Gregoire
Bristol & Manchester, Connecticut
49.5" x 49.5"

Our study quilt is based on the Eagle Medallion (c. 1840-1865) cover quilt from "Quilts and Quiltmakers Covering Connecticut". The original quilt was approximately 76" square. In order to meet the study requirements of a maximum 200" circumference, our first challenge was to reduce the amount of diamond rounds. Finding fabrics for the eagles, reducing the size of the appliqués to provide an overall balance, and trying to attain the correct light / dark fabrics for the star were also challenging.

Danbury Scott Fanton Museum and Historical Society, owner of the original quilt, was thrilled that the quilt was going to be reproduced. Brigid Guertin, executive director said, "We love this quilt. By reproducing the quilt for the AQSG Study, more people will see what a truly wonderful quilt it is."

This is our second AQSG Study quilt and since we are both Connecticut Yankees, we once again have chosen a quilt that originated from our state. This study has proved to be as much fun as the first time and we recommend the team process to everyone.

STARS FOR REBECCA

Beverly Birkmire
Chestertown, Maryland
33" x 38.5"

Several events motivated me to select the 1846 Rebecca Davis quilt as my inspiration. First was a workshop on hand-piecing the Le Moyne star, followed by my quilt guild's Repro Bee's choice of that star as a hand-piecing project. Then I visited the Metropolitan Museum of Art in New York. While there, I purchased the museum's book, "America's Quilts & Coverlets in the MMA" by Amelia Peck. The quilt featured on the cover caught my eye – Le Moyne stars.

I chose to create a smaller replica of the original quilt which measures 94" x 80", with 11 rows of nine stars across. The stars are about 8" square. I created 5" blocks arranged in seven rows of six blocks. My fabric choices echoed Rebecca's, with quite a few blue, brown, and striped fabrics. Dogtooth borders were appliquéd onto muslin. I hand quilted the piece using quilting motifs to mimic what I could see in the photo.

The first thing that occurred to me as I worked on the hand quilting was that I needed to have been more careful to trim excess fabric from the back of each block before beginning. Finishing the quilt with the very narrow binding of backing fabric rolled to the front was a new experience for me. Trimming of the front, batting, and backing prior to rolling the edge proved to be a bit tricky. Once done, however, rolling and stitching the edge were relatively easy.

Maker: Made by, Rebecca Davis. Pieced Quilt, ca. 1846. Cotton, 80 x 94 in. (203.2 cm x 238.8 cm).
Gift of Mrs. Andrew Galbraith Carey, 1980 (1980.498.3).

New England Stars

Claire McKarns
Encinitas, California
35" x 40"

The star blocks were purchased many years ago in New England. I have been saving these gems for a special occasion. Forty-two of the little pieces c. 1875 were used in this wallhanging. Each one is different.

The setting is similar to other old quilts from this time period.

The star blocks are checker-boarded with antique fabric from the same time period and set on the diagonal. Everything was hand stitched, sometimes using a 1/8" seam because the stars varied in size.

The borders and bindings are recent reproduction prints, mitered at the corners. I found the backing at a yard sale in Colorado in 2008, just before starting on this quilt. This helped me combine the best of old and new.

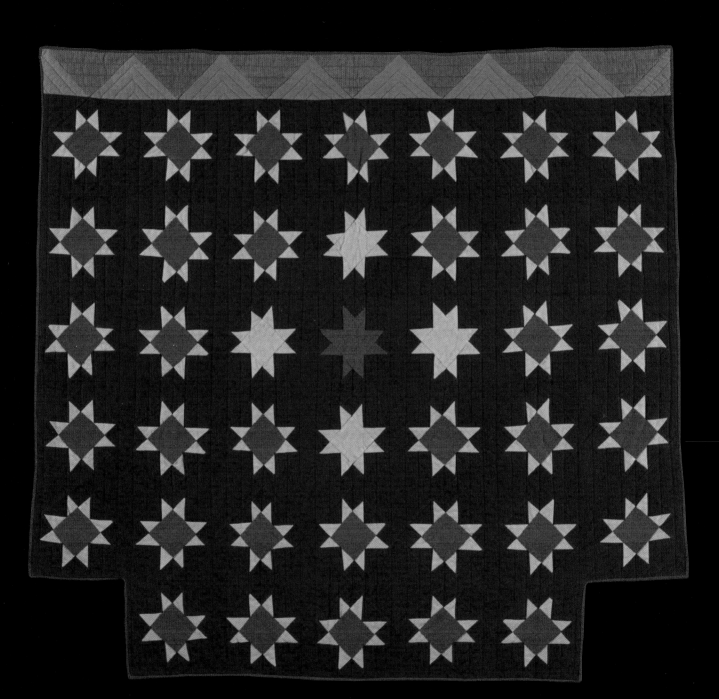

Courtesy of the Shelby Museum of History, Shelby, Ohio>>

STARS OVER MAINE

Sharon Pinka
Bellville, Ohio
49" x 49"

I first saw the inspiration quilt for my reproduction in 2009 while doing a documentation day at Shelby Old-Fashioned Days in Shelby, Ohio. Sally Maier, director of the local Shelby Historical Society, brought an enormous bundle to my table, unfolded the layers, and revealed an antique quilt unlike any I had ever seen. It was obviously very old, hand-dyed, -sewn, and -quilted, using homespun wool fabric, wool batting, and homespun linen backing. I estimated the age at c. 1800-1820, based on the style, fabric, and pattern.

The quilt measures 94" x 104" and has 36 - 10" red and gold star blocks, set on point, alternating with navy blue blocks, and brown and blue triangles at the quilt top. The lower corners were cut-out 30" to accommodate a four-poster bed.

According to Mrs. Maier, the quilt was donated to the museum in 1983 by Donna Hart, who stated it originally came from Warren, Maine. The quilt was given to her mother in 1958 by a Mrs. Cook, who died shortly after at age 92. There was speculation that it had belonged to the mother of one of her husband's ancestors, a Captain Cook. The time frame is incorrect for it to be the Captain Cook of Hawaii fame, but there are records of another Captain Cook who lived in Maine at a later time. This Captain Cook was probably a local man who sailed out of the Maine coast. Further genealogy research will be needed to pinpoint the family.

I chose to duplicate this one-quarter-sized quilt using flannel, cotton batting, and muslin backing. I changed the colors of the star combinations and reduced the size of the cut-out, since the original cut-outs appeared to have been done after the quilt was finished, and were asymmetrical. Sewing this quilt has given me a profound admiration for the unknown quilter who created these 17-piece stars, with their perfect points, glowing colors, and stitching which has lasted almost 200 years. Quilting was done by Jessica Carnes of Bellville, OH.

STAR MEDALLION: 200 YEARS LATER

Rägi Marino
Cedar Hill, Texas
48" x 48"

Le Moyne Stars were popular during the early 19th century, as was the use of central medallions. The intriguing aspect of the study quilt, owned by Denice Lipscomb, is the unusual manner in which these two elements are combined: the central medallion consists of 36 - 3" Le Moyne Stars. More often the central medallion is a single block and small [star] blocks are used in a border. Although the stars in the central medallion are of a single fabric, the remainder of the study quilt has a scrappy feel. No provenance is known about "Star Medallion," but the fabrics and style place it in the early 19th century.

After struggling with English paper piecing tiny Le Moyne Stars, I decided to paper piece standard eight pointed stars. I felt that in this case, the number of stars was more important than their style. Unable to find a reproduction fabric in the shade of blue used in the study quilt, a gold fabric from Jo Morton's "Harmonies" collection for Andover fabrics caught my eye. I used this for the medallion stars and as a basis for the color scheme of my quilt, which otherwise is a replica of the study quilt with only a few minor variations.

Mrs. Baldwin's Star

Joan Leahy Blanchard
West Townsend, Massachusetts
48" x 48"

I was taught Hexagon Patchwork as a child, by my very patient aunt who lived next door. Over the years I have been collecting and researching hexagon patterns. When the Star Challenge was announced by AQSG, I went to my own personal index. The one that stood out was a partially completed quilt in the book "Mosaic Patchwork" by Curious Press and Charleston Museum.

Mrs. Baldwin of North May River, SC apparently started this quilt between the years 1820 – 1830 but she never finished it. The center of the star featured a fussy cut design of pink fabric which was my inspiration for this challenge. My fabric choices were limited to five different fabrics, as was Mrs. Baldwin's. I chose to also fussy cut the centers of the rosettes and added an additional round of fabric to the rosettes.

Each tiny hexagon is 5/8" and there are 3,182 hexagons in the completed quilt.

I thank the Charleston Museum, Charleston, S.C., for granting permission for this project along with numerous photographs of this unfinished quilt.

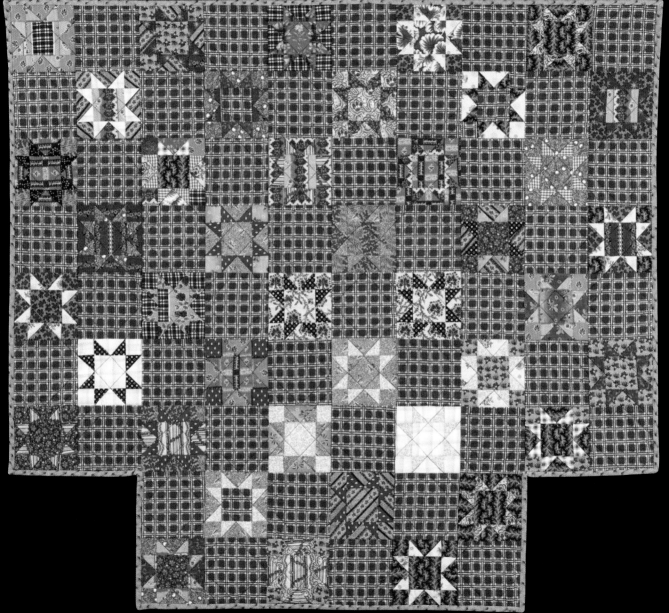

Collection of Jane Crutchfield

OH, MY, JANE!

Anita B. Loscalzo
Dover, Massachusetts
40" x 36"

The model for Oh, my, Jane! was purchased by Jane Crutchfield in 2008. It came from a home in Newburg, Maine, having spent the latter faded, tattered part of its life under a mattress over bed springs. I love its variety of 1840s fabrics randomly placed in many of the stars. My replica attempts to resurrect the exuberant colors of the original.

The original 80" x 72" quilt is composed of 82 – 8" square blocks with cut-out corners to accommodate a four-poster bed. The stars showcase the large variety of cotton textiles available in the 1840s. While the stars were randomly pieced from scraps from dress-making, the maker probably purchased the approximately 3 1/2 yards of brown plaid fabric expressly to make the quilt.

The replica's stars are composed of reproduction fabrics collected over years and the brown plaid from a closeout sale saved the project when I was despairing of finding anything close to the original. The back is plain muslin and printed cotton mimicking the wear of the original. The binding is a reproduction of Lane's Net, a best-seller among eccentrics popular from the 1820s to the 1840s.

Collection of Xenia Cord

STARS & SHAMROCKS 2

Xenia Cord
Kokomo, Indiana
43" x 49"

The Quilt Studies created for AQSG participants push me to try something new; each time I have been challenged (sometimes grudgingly) to work out of my comfort zone. The 2010 "Stars" project is no different.

I own the quilt that inspired this effort; despite a general aversion to appliqué, I have been intrigued by the methods used in the original. No perfectly pointed individual triangles for her: the multi-point stars are all single-cut pieces with blunt tips, as are the strips and arcs of triangles in the borders. The shamrocks and their curving stems are all single-cut. And despite having enough striped fabric for a better match in the borders, the original quiltmaker appears not to have been concerned about matching. That's my kind of quilter! Finally, the bright green original binding goes against our current passion for coordinated colors, and may have had some special meaning for her (or not).

The Jinny Beyer print used here was as close to the original c. 1820s buff, brown and teal stripe as I could find. Working out the appliqué was a minefield. NO machine stitching is involved. I hated making this little piece, but I'm glad I did it.

HUMBLE STAR

Marjorie J. Farquharson
Needham, Massachusetts
44" x 44"

Whenever I look for inspiration from 19th century quilters, I am drawn to quilts that speak to me either because of pattern, color, or fabric. The quilt that I chose to interpret is one that I've looked at many times in "Small Endearments" by Sandi Fox. It appealed to me because of the complexity of the center and the colors and varieties of fabric. I've named it "Humble Star" because of the intricacy of the center star that is surrounded by simple blocks. I wonder whether the original quilter made that center block and decided that she wouldn't make any other stars. Another possibility could be that a second quilter took the center star and finished it in a quilt. The most interesting possibility to me is that original quilter wanted the quilt to come out just as it is from the beginning. Whichever scenario is closest to reality; this was an interesting project to complete.

From the collection of Pat L. Nickols

STARS UPON STARS ALL AROUND

Kay Triplett
Spring, Texas
48" x 52"

I was inspired by a quilt which hung at the 2009 AQSG Seminar in San Jose, California. It was in the main ballroom and each day I became more and more interested in learning what it took to make a quilt with nearly 2,000 diamonds and more bias edges than I could count. I am not sure of how the original quilt was pieced, but I chose to do English paper piecing for the center star, then resorted to faster strip piecing methods and a sewing machine for other parts of the quilt.

Adding to my challenge is that I had to make the quilt half scale to comply with the size restrictions for the Study. While 1840s reproduction prints are readily available, most of them are not half scale. I did my best to match the fabrics from the quilt, while favoring the fabrics designed by Pat L. Nickols, owner of the quilt. Friends who have seen the quilt have marveled at the color choices, often thinking I must have changed them to give the quilt more impact. I can say that the color choices were made 170 years ago, and that she must have been a woman like me, interested in mathematics, precision and art.

Northern Lights

Didi Salvatierra
Bel Air, Maryland
46.5" x 46.5"

My quilt is an adaptation of a 19th century pieced star pattern identified in Barbara Brackman's "Encyclopedia of Pieced Quilt Patterns", on page 217, as Cluster of Stars - LAC #393. The original publication date is stated as 1897.

I won the original quilt for $10 at a guild meeting, when someone brought in the quilt saying it "needed to go to a good home." The guild held a spontaneous raffle and I was the winner!

What drew me to the quilt was the dense hand quilting that I saw from the back side, folded up in someone's arms. I am glad I paid attention!

My original plan was to reproduce this quilt in a new pattern and teach it as a workshop. As I began piecing the stars, I felt their scale too small and the piecing too tedious to keep students interested. So the result is this one quilt. I admire the tenacity of the original quiltmaker to see her quilt to completion; it is bed size.

My vision for this quilt was to reproduce the quilting and the proportions of the original but make it in more contemporary fabrics/colors. Fortunately, the quilting designs used in the original are still available commercially so I did not have to create my own stencils. I chose two colors of quilting thread; yellow to enhance the "pretty" quilting and a blue/purple variegated for the fill in lines. I am pleased that my quilting in this quarter size quilt retains the denseness of quilting.

I used a variety of yellow fabrics for the stars and repeated this mix on the border. The addition of piping gives a nice finish to the outer edge of the quilt.

Courtesy The Quilt Complex, Albion, CA

STARBURST

Janet Locey
Hollister, California
Machine quilted by Holly Casey
35" x 35"

When I walked into the Special Exhibit at American Quilt Study Group Seminar in San Jose, California, I knew immediately my search was over and I'd found a very unusual star quilt for my 2010 study quilt.

"Starburst," owned by Julie Silber, was made by Amanda Dubois for her grandson Andrew Dubois for a wedding gift in Ashville, North Carolina and dated 1878. Pieced stars appliquéd onto a strip pieced background and lots of embroidery graces this quilt.

The original quilt was 75" x 75." I reconstructed the quilt on a small scale using modern techniques. The stars were fused onto a pieced background and embellished with free motion machine embroidery and a small machine blanket stitch. Even with modern techniques this project was a huge undertaking with over 2,000 yards of thread used for the embroidery.

The study quilt is made with cotton fabric. The original quilt was made with silk and wool at the beginning of the Crazy Quilt period. Although the piecing is very symmetrical, the elaborate embroidery work could have been influenced by a Japanese fan quilt. Embroidery work on crazy quilts was just coming into fashion when this quilt was made in 1878. The 1876 Philadelphia Centennial Exposition with the Japanese Exhibit is credited for inspiring crazy quilting in the United States.

BLUE STAR

Sherry Burkhalter
Newville, Alabama
48" x 48"

A star quilt ...from Alabama ...with a story behind it ... was the criteria for choosing my quilt.

In a lecture by Mary Elizabeth Johnson Huff about her Alabama quilt documentation, she told of a quilt found in Selma with an incredible story.

Miss Jones' family of French ancestry owned a cotton plantation in the early 1800s in Marion. A "mysterious occurrence" caused the father to move the family to Selma, and they never intended to return. They disinterred their ancestors and reburied them in Selma. As hard times became a fact of life after the Civil War, his daughter taught needlework. This quilt, made some 40 years earlier, was surely a teaching piece.

A visit to Mrs. Huff's allowed me to view the quilt. I enlarged my picture using a copier. I hand applied the fleur-de-lis embellished star in the center medallion onto tea-dyed fabric. It was set in a larger, machine-pieced star (a challenge to get the angles just right). Surrounded by Stars of Le Moyne and a rope-style border, the star is set on point, and corners filled with "clamshells" (my first attempt) to make a square. The quilt is finished with borders of Stars of Le Moyne and foundation-pieced slender diamonds.

PISTACHIOS, CHERRIES AND CHOCOLATE

Catherine Noll Litwinow
Bettendorf, Iowa
36" x 58"

I bookmarked the "World's Wonder" quilt when I got the "Nebraska Quilts & Quiltmakers", edited by Patricia Cox Crews and Ronald C. Naugle. I was drawn to the double pinks in the quilt. I would like to imagine that Armina stitched some of the stars traveling through Iowa.

Winnifred Petersen and I attended many Iowa Quilters Guild programs. I drove around the state while Winnifred basted her tiny hexagons.

The fabric makers certainly helped by producing many chocolate and cherry colored fabrics. The fun part came in selecting the fabrics for the five rows.

I paper-pieced the hexagons and triangles. Each motif has 37 hexagons and the 73 triangles.

There are many stars in the quilt. After being told the quilt was a part of the "Star Study," quilting friends immediately saw the stars. The triangles around each hexagon form a star and also the large white triangles make bigger stars.

FENCE RAIL STAR

Virginia Berger
Adel, Iowa
48" x 48"

The quilt I used for inspiration is made of 9 blocks of the pattern, Fence Row Star or Log Cabin Star (Brackman #3749) that was published by Hearth and Home magazine. I've always found it interesting that only one of the nine blocks is pieced correctly! I wanted to examine how the block might have been pieced and what could have confused the maker. While searching for information about the block from different sources and a couple of other quilts of this pattern in the Quilt Index, I discovered some ambiguity about color placement in the block that I also explored. I used modified strip piecing techniques to make this block. It still took focus to get the right color in the right place—I can really understand how someone using template cut pieces could have become confused! It was interesting to explore the construction of this block and you have to admire the original maker's persistence. She may have been confused—but she got a quilt done to keep her family warm!

VARIABLE STAR REVISITED

June McCauley Ross
Georgetown, South Carolina
42" x 42"

I had previously participated in the "Red and Green" study and found it extremely gratifying. So when the new subject was announced I immediately began planning what I might do. Firstly, I wanted to reflect the heritage of South Carolina. I went to Laurel Horton's book, "Social Fabric" and found a picture of a star quilt made in S.C. in 1870. It really appealed to me because it had an appliquéd medallion in the center. Unfortunately, the photograph was black and white and I had no idea of the colors used. I went on the Internet and found the oldest chintz that I could and relied on the accuracy of reproduction fabric of the period to duplicate the quilt as best I could. I wanted to create a vintage look so I used stained muslin to complete the project. Beads were added for a little sparkle...........upon finishing the piece I was struck by the fact that how timeless star quilts are and that they have provided a continuity throughout history even as radical changes have occurred in so many other areas.

RED & GREEN STARS

Joy Swartz
Prescott, Arizona
45" x 45"

I first laid eyes on my inspiration quilt while walking through the booths at an antique show in Nashville, TN. While I own a number of red/green quilts, none were pieced, and few matched this quilting. I kept walking back and forth in front of the booth trying to figure out if I could copy it, as I found the pattern so appealing. Finally my husband, getting a bit weary of this, asked why I didn't just go buy it. End of story. I love this quilt hung on a wall. It is so graphic in its design plus the knockout punch, for me, is when one gets close enough to see that the quilting which extends throughout the quilt, never leaves more than a 1/4" unquilted.

With the help of my husband, I created a graph to make the quilt half the size of the original. While her quilt had one inch half-square triangles, mine would have 1/2" half-square triangles. I decided I wanted the challenge of reproducing her quilt exactly as she had made it, initially including her extensive quilting.

I have become quite humbled while making this quilt. I like large challenges, which is certainly what I got with this one. Even with paper piecing, my quilt has points that don't point. HER quilt has every point pointing. I have not followed her quilting patterns in their entirety; there simply weren't enough hours in the day to allow me to quilt this miniature to the extent she quilted her larger one. I started out quilting it at half scale of hers, and found that quilting 1/8" apart (hers is 1/4" apart) blurred the patterns she had made.

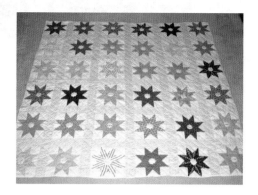

STAR SIGNATURE QUILT

Susan Price Miller
Pella, Iowa
42" x 52"

I studied an unusual pieced star signature quilt in my collection dated 1877. The 36 10" blocks probably came from northern New Jersey, the home of most of the signers, and were joined with wide sashing a generation later.

The center points of the stars are cut away in convex curves, providing space for signatures. I discovered a small group of published examples of similar eight and six pointed stars. All have narrow sashing and borders and were made in the New York/New Jersey area before the Civil War.

Unlike typical late-19th century Midwestern quilts available to me, my quilt contains Eastern fabrics with lighter or clearer colors. Finding period reproduction fabrics was difficult because so many are dark or grayed. My new version has 20 - 8" blocks with examples of simple geometric designs and refined small figures made from reproductions, older stashed fabrics, and`a vintage solid pink almost identical to the one from 1877. The narrow red print sashing and border are reminders of the pre-Civil War star signature quilts.

I learned about the history of my quilt and the star pattern. I also gained an appreciation for a wider variety of fabrics available in the 1870s.

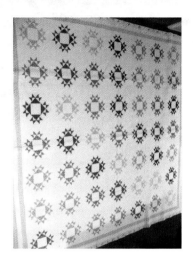

AULT STAR

Karen Dever
Moorestown, New Jersey
33" x 33"

My first trip to an American Quilt Study Group Seminar was in 2005 in Colorado. What an unreal experience – I met so many people and learned so much from the study centers and tours that I took. One of the events during the seminars is the ability to shop at the vendors. What a shock to see such wonderful textiles! I purchased the quilt that I have used as my inspiration for this seminar study. The unusual star and the detailed quilting drew my attention immediately.

The quilt is an unusual star block that I have not been able to find a name for in any of my research of quilt blocks. One corner on the back of the original quilt has a signature but the entire name is not clear. It reads as "Je..me..a Ault". I was told that the quilt came from Ohio when I made the purchase. Upon returning home, I did further research on Ancestry.com and found out that in the late 1890s, 90 percent of all people living in the USA with the last name of Ault lived in Ohio. The quilt has several characteristics of an Ohio quilt.

I named this block The Ault Star due to the signature and no other information.

The original quilt inspired this small wallhanging.

HOMESPUN STAR

Greta VanDenBerg-Nestle
Oak Shade, Pennsylvania
36" x 36"

Initially, I planned to use a quilt in my own collection as inspiration for the Quilt Study until this long-time favorite jumped off the page of my well-loved copy of "Treasury of American Quilts", by Cyril I. Nelson and Carter Houck. As co-chair of the AQSG Quilt Study project, I reasoned that changing my original plan would give me an opportunity to do what other participants were being asked to do: seek permission to use images of the inspiration pieces used for the Quilt Study.

My only disappointment in the process came when I learned from the Museum of American Folk Art, the current owner of the 'Center Star Quilt', that there is very little provenance available for this amazing bedcover. After reviewing what is known, it became obvious the information had evolved as quilt historians learned more about identification of fibers used in early whole cloth quilts. For example, the fabrics in this quilt are identified as linsey-woolsey in one publication and wool in another. The confusion about early fabrics gave me just the inspiration I needed; I decided to investigate the process of how 'home' spun and woven fibers used in early quilts would have been produced.

My journey started with the purchase of a 19th century spinning wheel. I had never spun any type of fiber before. I found the process very challenging in the beginning, initially believing I would never be able to produce a yarn consistently fine enough to actually create fabric. However, with a pound of perseverance I succeeded in spinning enough wool to weave all of the fabrics in my quilt. The front is 100% wool from sheep raised near my home in Lancaster County, Pennsylvania. For contrast I opted to create 'linsey-woolsey' by weaving a wool weft through a purchased linen warp for the back of the quilt.

As a result of making 'Homespun Star', I have a genuine appreciation for the industrial revolution that helped relieve women of the responsibility to create the fabrics needed by their families and in their homes. Notwithstanding the hours required to create a few inches of genuine homespun fabric, I am inspired to spin all of the wools and linens to make a whole cloth bed quilt the old fashioned way.

In Memoriam: Elizabeth passed away after completing her quilt.

EVENING STAR

Elizabeth M. Pappius
Brookline, Massachusetts
54.5" x 66"

Why this quilt? The inspiration quilt for my "Evening Star" immediately caught my eye when I saw it on Stella Rubin's website. It contained several elements that I particularly like: star blocks, an on-point setting, a scrappy style, and beautiful Turkey red and madder fabrics. My stash of antique fabrics included many pieces of antique Turkey red and madder prints, and I was eager to use them.

Approach/design. I decided that my quilt would be smaller than the inspiration quilt, and that it would be made entirely by hand. I had to back into the dimensions of the blocks and the sashing to keep the proportions similar to the inspiration quilt. I was fortunate to find several beautiful reproduction turkey red fabrics, and used one for the sashing, another for the border, and a third for the back.

What I learned. I learned a lot about the geometry of working backward from the desired finished size of a star block to the size of its individual pieces, as well as how to create the triangular blocks around the perimeter. I deviated from the inspiration quilt in making my perimeter blocks smaller than an exact half of the square blocks. I also opted to add a border, using a border print that was not symmetrical either horizontally or vertically. It took me many tries to create mirror image border corners while minimizing "fudging" along the sides. I also learned how to make round appliqué pieces for the centers.

Starlight Pathways

Bonita J. Morley
Saratoga, California
41.5" x 44"

My inspirational moment came when I first saw the picture of Rolling Star (in "Repiecing the Past" by Sara Dillow). I recognized color and pattern played an important role in the making of this quilt. The initial color combination seemed unusual to me. Perhaps the maker of this quilt used fabric colors which altered the coloring of the original greens, pinks, blues, and brownish mustard. How could I learn by modifying the original quilt pattern? Should I use darker as well as lighter colors to create a new version of this Rolling Star pattern?

I realized that the block patterns varied in scale and size. There were 12" blocks with eight star points; 4" blocks with 8 "mini" star points and 4" x 12" sashing pieces connecting the mini/stars to the diagonal lattice effect.

Finally, the moment came when I saw that the 4" sashing could be triple-pieced by designing lighter as well as darker colors within the 4" sashing borders. The pathway was finally clear for me to see!

STARS!
PATTERNS

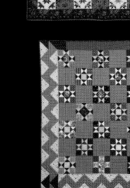

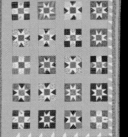

CHEDDAR STARS OVER MOAB

Sandra Starley
Moab, Utah
21" x 24"

I love the joyful c. 1885 cheddar orange and double pink color scheme and I knew this star design would be fun to make. I found the quilt charming with its uneven stars and the dogtooth border on only two sides.

This is my second version - first was for a current fabric line fundraiser challenge and it was fun to make the old quilt in new funky fabrics. But I decided to try again with half size blocks (3" rather than 6") and reproduction fabrics. I strove for exact matches to the antique fabric and it was interesting to see what I could find - I learned a lot about browns c. 1860-1890. I chose to foundation piece my stars and was careful to replicate the angular lines of the plaids and stripes which give the quilt movement.

The maker and I share a sense of playful quilting. I feel a kinship with anyone who isn't afraid of using a lot of cheddar orange but I'm a bit more persnickety. The maker used a variety of techniques - hand quilting and hand appliqué, all machine binding and machine appliqué. It is always enlightening to see how another quilter addressed the same challenges and what they accomplished without rotary cutters and all the other gadgets we 'must have'.

CHEDDAR STARS OVER MOAB

Instructions are for a quilt that measures 20 1/2" x 25".

Fabric needed

- 3/8 yard solid light for star points and border triangles
- 1/4 yard printed light for star backgrounds
- 1/4 yard dark for star backgrounds
- 1/4 yard medium for star centers and inner border (double pinks)
- 5/8 yard medium for sashing (cheddar)

Cutting

Stars

- Cut 20 - 1 1/2" medium center squares.
- Cut 124 - 1 1/2" dark squares.
- Cut 36 -1 1/2" printed light squares.
- Cut 80 - 1 3/4" solid light squares; cut the squares diagonally once to make 160 triangles.

Sashing

- A - Cut 16 rectangles, 3 1/2" x 2".
- B - Cut 8 rectangles, 3 1/2" x 1 3/4".
- C - Cut 3 rectangles, 23 1/2" x 2".
- D - Cut 2 rectangles, 23 1/2" x 2 1/2".
- E - Cut 1 rectangle, 20 1/2" x 2".

Inner border

- Cut 1 rectangle, 23 1/4" x 1".
- Cut 1 rectangle, 17 1/4" x 1".
- Cut 13 solid light squares, 1 1/4"; cut the squares diagonally to make 26 triangles.

To sew the star block

Star points

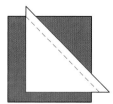

- *Note: these star points are not uniform. To make the slightly unconventional stars, follow these steps that have been adapted from the Liberated Stars method described by Gwen Marston and Freddy Moran in Collaborative Quilting, Sterling Publishing Co., 2006, pp. 180-81.*

1. With the square right side up, place a solid light triangle on the right side of the square. The placement of the triangle on the square above is illustrative only; slight variations in the placement will make the star points non-uniform, which is what you want.

2. Sew the triangle to the square by stitching parallel to the triangle's hypotenuse (long side).

3. Press the triangle back over the stitching line.

4. Trim the triangle to the size of the square.

5. With the square right side up, place a solid light triangle on the left side of the square.

6. Repeat the stitching, pressing, and trimming.

Block Assembly

- Sew the units into 3 rows. Sew the rows together.
- #For 4 of the star blocks, use printed light squares where # appears.
- *For 5 of the star blocks, use printed light squares where * appears.
- Make 20 blocks.

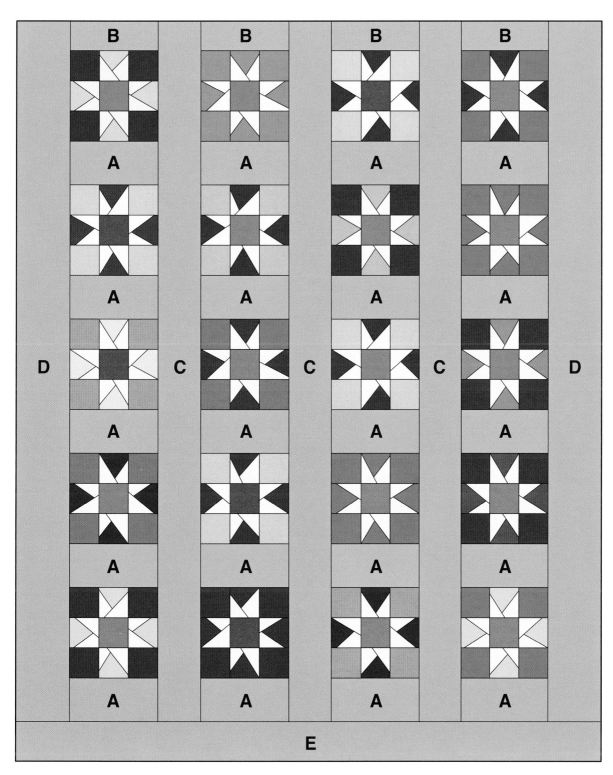

Assembly Diagram

To assemble the quilt top

1. Sew a rectangle A to each of 16 star blocks.

2. Sew a rectangle B to each of the remaining 4 star blocks, and sew a rectangle B on the opposite side from rectangle A on 4 other star blocks.

3. Arrange the star/rectangle units according to the Assembly Diagram and sew them into 4 columns.

4. Arrange the star/rectangle columns with C rectangles between them and D rectangles on the outsides. Sew the columns and rectangles together.

5. Sew rectangle E to one end of the quilt top.

Inner Border Appliqué

- Press under seam allowances on one long side and one short side of each triangle. (The third edge will be covered.)
- Press under seam allowances on the 17 1/4" x 1" and 23 1/4" x 1" rectangles.

Bottom Inner Border

1. With the unpressed edge of each triangle parallel with the bottom edge of the quilt top, space 8 triangles across the bottom border. Place the unpressed edges of the triangles 1 1/4" from the bottom edge of the quilt top; the triangle on the right 3" from the side edge; and the triangle on the left 2 1/2" from the side edge.

2. Appliqué the triangles onto the quilt top.

3. Position the 17 1/4" x 1" rectangle over the unpressed triangle edges, 1 1/8" from the bottom edge of the quilt top and 2" from the left side edge.

4. Machine stitch the rectangle to the quilt top, sewing very closely to the edge of the rectangle with matching thread.

Side inner border

1. With the unpressed edge of each of the remaining triangles parallel with the right side edge of the quilt top, space 18 triangles along the side border. Place the unpressed edges of the triangles 1" from the side edge of the quilt top; the triangle on the right 7/8" from the top edge; and the triangle on the left 1 5/8" from the bottom edge. The triangles of the side inner border will be closer together than the triangles of the bottom inner border.

2. Appliqué the triangles onto the quilt top.

3. Position the rectangle over the unpressed triangle edges, 3/4" from the side edge of the quilt top and even with the inner border rectangle on the bottom border.

4. Machine stitch the rectangle to the quilt top.

Finishing

- Assemble the backing, batting, and top. Baste together. Quilt by machine or hand. Bind.

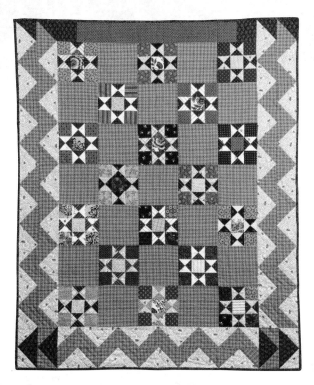

DEBORAH'S STAR

Carolyn Maruggi
Hilton, New York
42.5" x 51"

As a volunteer at the Rochester Historical Society, I had the privilege of helping a dedicated group of women document and re-house the Society's quilt collection, thus giving me several star quilts from which to choose. What attracted me to this c. 1840 **Ohio Star** was the opportunity to research the maker whose initials, **DC**, (Deborah A. Carpenter) are cross-stitched on the back. Rosemary Webster Smith (1916-1987) gave the quilt to the Society in 1986.

I decided to try and replicate the **look** of the quilt in a smaller size. Scaling the blocks was not a problem. The zigzag border, however, was a challenge. After re-doing the zigzags for a second time I had newfound respect for Deborah Ann who worked her magic without graph paper, a rotary cutter or plastic rulers.

I have found a Deborah A. Carpenter (1824-1909) who may have been the quiltmaker but I haven't been able to find a family connection between Deborah and Rosemary. Deborah was born in 1824 in New Rochelle, Westchester County, NY. Rosemary Smith is buried in Westchester County. Deborah married George Hall, Jr. on 30 October 1846, in New York City. They had one son. She lived in Westchester County all of her life. Both women had family connections in Rochester, NY. It's possible the connection is through Rosemary's husband, William Arthur Smith.

It's a time consuming challenge but I have not given up my search.

Deborah's Star

Instructions are for a quilt that measures 42" x 51".

Fabric Requirements

- Scraps for 18 Ohio Star blocks
- 1 1/4 yards gold plaid for setting blocks and pieced border
- 2/3 yard tan print for pieced border
- 1/4 yard dark red print for pieced border
- 1/4 yard red print for top border
- 1/2 yard blue print for binding

Cutting Directions

For each Ohio Star block (18 total), cut:

- 4 – 2 1/2" squares for corners (note 2 blocks contain a renegade square of a different fabric)
- 1 – 2 1/2" square for center
- 2 – 3 1/4" square of light, cut twice on the diagonal to make 8 triangles for star points
- 2 – 3 1/4" square of darker, cut twice on the diagonal to make 8 triangles for star points

From gold plaid, cut:

- 17 – 6 1/2" squares for setting blocks
- 5 – 7 1/4" squares, cut twice on the diagonal to make 20 triangles for border (discard one extra)
- 22 – 3 7/8" squares, cut once on the diagonal to make 44 triangles for border

From tan print, cut:

- 5 – 7 1/4" squares, cut twice on the diagonal to make 20 triangles for border (discard one extra)
- 22 – 3 7/8" squares, cut once on the diagonal to make 44 triangles for border

From dark red print, cut:

- 1 – 7 1/4" squares, cut twice on the diagonal to make 4 triangles for border
- 2 – 3 7/8" squares, cut once on the diagonal to make 4 triangles for border
- 2 – 3 1/2" squares for border

From red print, cut:

- 1 – 3 1/2" strip (see Quilt Assembly, Step 4)

Make Blocks

- Stitch a light triangle to a darker triangle. Make 8 identical units. Stitch together 2 units to make 4 - 2 1/2" unfinished half-square triangles for star points.

Make 8

Make 4

- Refer to the block diagram and make 18 Ohio Star blocks.

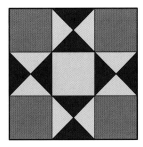

Make 18

Make Flying Geese Border Blocks

- Stitch a tan print triangle to each side of a large gold plaid triangle to make a 6 1/2" x 3 1/2" unfinished flying geese unit.

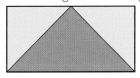

Make:

- 19 flying geese units using a large gold plaid triangle with tan print triangles.
- 19 flying geese units using a large tan print triangle with small gold plaid triangles.
- 2 flying geese units using a large dark red triangle with small tan print triangles.
- 2 flying geese units using a large dark red triangle with small gold plaid triangles.

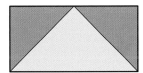

Make 19

Make 19

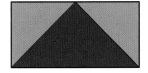

Make 2

Make 2

• Stitch the flying geese units together as shown and make 6 1/2" unfinished border blocks.

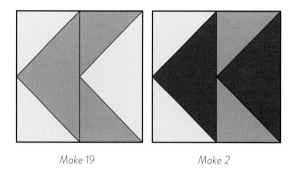

Make 19   Make 2

Make Half-Square Triangles Border Blocks

• Stitch triangles together to make 3 1/2" unfinished half-square triangles.

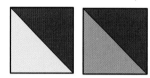

Make 2 of each

Quilt Assembly

1. Lay out the center of the quilt, alternating an Ohio Star block with a gold plaid setting block making 7 rows of 5 blocks each. Refer to the assembly diagram. Stitch each row together, pressing the seams towards the setting blocks. Stitch the rows together.

2. Refer to the assembly diagram and stitch together 2 side borders, each with 7 tan print/gold plaid flying geese border blocks. Be sure the blocks are turned properly to form the zigzag border. Stitch a border to each side, making sure the blocks in the quilt center are sewn to a tan print.

3. Stitch together the remaining 5 tan print/gold plaid flying geese border blocks to make the bottom border. Be sure the blocks are turned properly to form the zigzag border. Refer to the assembly diagram and stitch a dark red/tan print/gold plaid flying geese border block to each end. Stitch to the bottom of the quilt.

4. For the top border, refer to the assembly diagram and stitch together a tan print/dark red print half-square triangle border block to a gold/plaid half-square triangle border block. Next add a 3 1/2" dark red print square for the left side of the top border. For the right end unit, stitch together a 3 1/2" dark red print square to a tan print/dark red print half-square triangle border block. Next add a gold plaid/dark red half-square triangle border block for the right side of the top border. Trim the 3 1/2" strip of red to 24 1/2" (or the measurement needed for your quilt). Add the proper 3 block unit to each side of the red strip. Stitch to the top of the quilt.

Finishing

- Quilt as desired and bind.

Assembly Diagram

STAR OF ENGLAND

Cindy Vermillion Hamilton
Pagosa Springs, Colorado
40" x 49"

On a trip to England in 2006, I discovered an old quilt in an antique store. Despite its tattered and poor condition, I was fascinated by it because of its age and the circular blocks. While studying UK quilts, I have rarely found examples of repeat blocks that constitute the entire quilt top, as we so commonly find in America. I knew I needed to rescue the quilt and make a modern version to document it and save the unusual pattern from extinction.

The blocks appear to be several years older than the border, which was added later by machine. While searching out similar fabrics, I drafted the block in the same size as the original piece, and then I reduced it. A goal was to learn the finishing technique we refer to as "knife edge", the most common way antique UK quilts were finished. I was able to work out a method that produced very satisfactory and authentic results.

This quilt illustrates the difficulty American historians have in dating early English prints. Fabrics in the original quilt are similar to those in other UK quilts dating to about 1825, but many would be dated later by American historians, to about 1840. This project really helped me to focus on this discrepancy between dates of fabrics used in quilts from America and the UK. I felt a deep connection to the original maker as I stitched. How thrilled she would be to see her design honored by this AQSG quilt study project.

Star of England

Instructions are for a quilt that measures 40" x 47 1/2".

Fabric Needed

- 7/8 yard light fabric
- 1/8 yard each of 20 assorted medium and dark fabrics
- 1 1/4 yard for borders

Cutting   Note: Templates are on page 77.

- A — Cut 160 from assorted medium and dark fabrics (8 pieces from each fabric).
- B — Cut 160 from light fabric.
- C — Cut 160 from assorted medium and dark fabrics (8 pieces from each fabric).
- D — Cut 160 from light fabric.
- E — Cut 80 from assorted medium and dark fabrics (4 pieces from each fabric). Reverse E and cut 80 from assorted medium and dark fabrics (4 pieces from each fabric).

Block Assembly

1. Sew A to B. Press toward dark fabric.

2. Sew another A to the A in Step 1. Press.

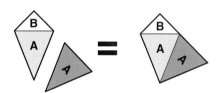

3. Repeat Step 1 three more times, orienting A and B units the same each time. Sew the units together to create a square.

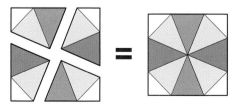

4. Sew B to the short side of C. Press toward dark fabric.

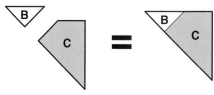

5. Sew D to the long side of another C. Press toward dark fabric.

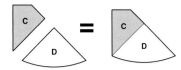

6. Sew the units from Step 4 and Step 5 together. Make 3 more.

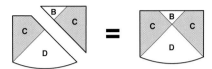

7. Sew 2 of the units from Step 6 to opposite sides of square from Step 3.

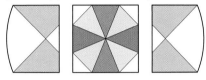

8. On 2 of the units from Step 6, sew D to each end. Press toward dark fabric.

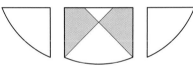

9. Sew 2 units from Step 8 to unit from Step 7, matching up seams and creating a circle.

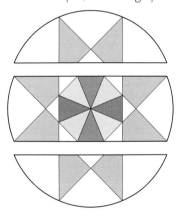

10. Sew 8 Es together, alternating the orientation of the E pieces, creating a frame.

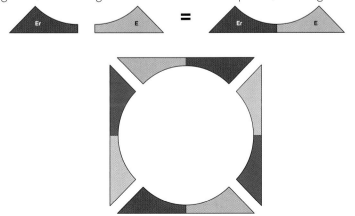

11. Pin the circle from Step 9 inside frame from Step 10, matching seam and easing in fullness. Sew circle to frame. Press toward frame.

- Make 20 blocks.

Quilt Assembly

1. Arrange 20 blocks in 5 rows of 4 blocks.

2. Sew the rows together, matching seams. Press.

3. Measure the middle of the long side blocks unit.

4. Cut 2 rectangles from the border fabric 5 1/2" x length of long side + 1/2". Sew to the long sides, matching centers and easing fullness. Press toward the border.

5. Measure the middle of the short side of blocks unit with borders added.

6. Cut 2 rectangles from border fabric 5 1/2" x length of short side + 1/2". Sew to the short sides and previous borders, matching centers and easing fullness. Press toward the border. *Note: Borders may be pieced, depending on the width of the fabric. If so, include additional length for the seam allowances.*

Finishing

- Assemble the backing, batting, and top and baste together. Quilt by machine or hand. Turn in the edges of top and back to make a knife edge and stitch closed.

Knife edge binding

- "Knife edge" binding is a technique where no binding shows on the front of the quilt. It takes skill to keep the edge straight and even. This quilt, and several others, is bound to simulate that style.

To add a knife edge binding:

- Cut binding strips from the same fabric as the backing, 1 1/2" wide. Join the strips – you will need about 185" of binding (5 strips joined).Attach the first side of the binding to the front of the quilt, using a 1/4" seam allowance. Trim the batting after attaching the binding, then turn the entire binding to the back of the quilt. Turn under half the binding width and hand stitch with a blind stitch to the back, mitering at the corners as you go around the quilt.

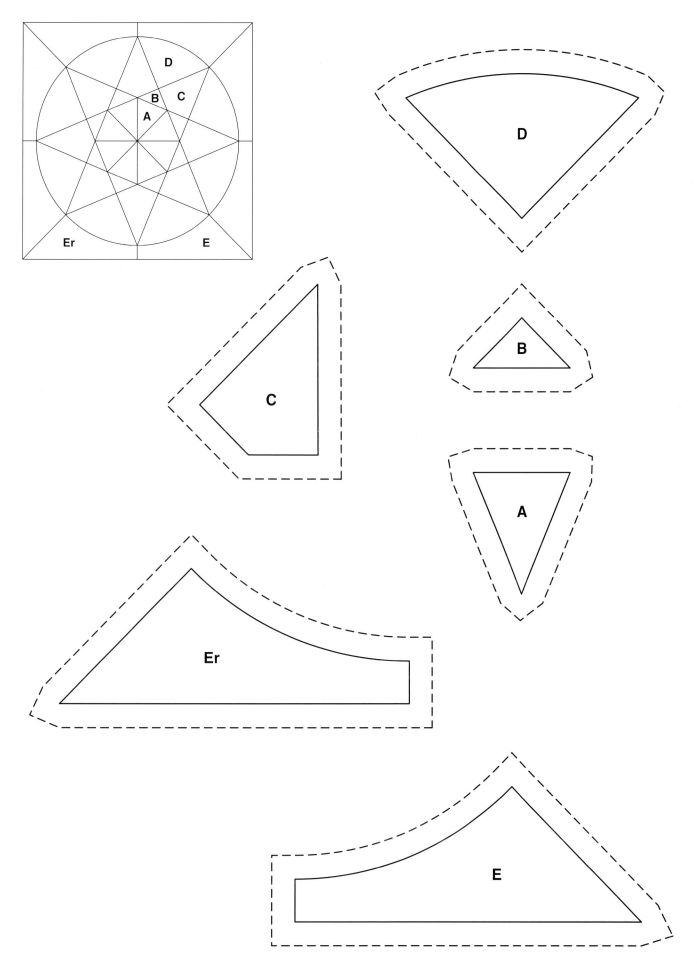

D

B

C

A

Er

E

Collection of the New England Quilt Museum

Eight-Pointed Star — Borden Family Quilt

Florence McConnell
Twaine Harte, California
41.5" x 37.25"

My study quilt is in the collection of the New England Quilt Museum and pictured in two books – "The New England Quilt Museum Quilts" by Jennifer Gilbert and "Massachusetts Quilts" by Lynne Bassett. I love early chintz prints and found the pillar border fabric and the cutout corner design of this particular quilt striking. I selected reproduction fabrics as my intent was to duplicate the quilt as closely as possible. The majority of piecing was done by hand, then hand quilted similar to the original. The eight-pointed star (commonly called Le Moyne Star) and sawtooth border construction were particularly challenging but rewarding, once completed.

Reproducing this quilt gave me an appreciation for the maker of this complex and large quilt. I visualized a woman with the leisure time to pursue her craft, the resources to purchase such expensive fabric in the early 19th century, and a family who treasured the quilt since it continues to be in excellent condition.

According to the published information, this quilt was found in the home of Lizzie Borden's great-uncle, Cook Borden, and was thought to have been made in the first quarter of the 19th century. Mr. Borden was, in fact, considered a wealthy man. Many of us recall the rhyme, **"Lizzie Borden took an axe and gave her mother 40 whacks"**. From this rhyme, I always assumed Lizzie had been convicted of the crime. Doing a little research on the family, I found she was actually acquitted in court!

EIGHT-POINTED STAR —BORDEN FAMILY QUILT

Instructions are for a quilt that measures 42" x 37 1/2".

Fabric Requirements

- 1 yard light for star backgrounds for blocks, sashing cornerstones, and outer border triangles
- 1/3 yard dark for star diamonds
- 1/3 yard medium for star diamonds
- 1/3 yard print for sashing rectangles
- 1/4 yard dark for outer border triangles
- 3/4 yard print for final borders
- 1/3 yard for binding

Cutting Directions

Template is on page 83.

From the light, cut:

- 86 – 1 3/4" squares (B) for background corners of the blocks and the sashing cornerstones
- 21 – 3" squares, cut twice on the diagonal to make 84 (C) triangles for background triangles of the blocks
- 10 – 3" squares, cut twice on the diagonal to make 40 (D) triangles for background setting triangles for half-blocks and sashing setting triangles
- 1 – 2" square, cut once on the diagonal, to make 2 (E) triangles for corner setting triangles
- 8 – 4 1/4" squares, cut twice on the diagonal to make 32 triangles for outer border (only 30 are needed)
- 2 – 3 7/8" squares, cut once on the diagonal to make 4 outer border corner triangles

From the dark (for stars), cut:

- 84 diamonds using template A

From the medium (for stars), cut:

- 84 diamonds using template A

From the print (sashing), cut:

- 42 – 1 3/4" x 4 3/4" rectangles for sashing

From the dark, cut:

- 9 – 4 1/4" squares, cut twice on the diagonal to make 36 triangles for outer border (only 34 are needed)

From the print, cut:

- 3 – 7 1/2" strips for final borders

Star Block Assembly

Note: these instructions are for 1 block.

- Stitch together a dark diamond and a light diamond as shown. Make 4.

- Stitch the 4 units together to form the star.

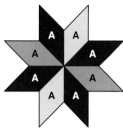

- Inset 4 light B squares on the corners of the block. Inset 4 light C triangles to complete the star block. Make 15 blocks.

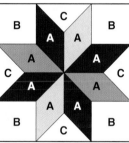

Star Half Block Assembly

- Stitch together a dark diamond and a light diamond as shown. Make 2.

- Stitch the 2 units together to form half of a star.

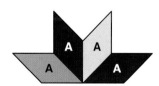

- Inset a light B squares on the corner of the block. Inset 2 light C triangles. Stitch a D triangle to each side to complete the star block. Make 11 blocks.

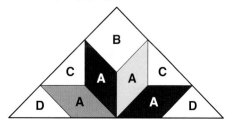

Star Setting Triangle Assembly

- Stitch together a dark diamond and a light diamond as shown.

- Inset a light C triangle between the star diamonds. Stitch a light D triangle to each side to complete the star setting triangle. Make 2 blocks.

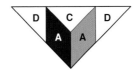

Inner Quilt Assembly

- Refer to the Assembly Diagram. Lay out the star blocks, print sashing and light cornerstones (B). Put the half star blocks and the light sashing setting triangles (D) in place along the sides, top and bottom. A star setting triangle goes in each top corner and a light corner setting triangle (E) in each lower corner. Stitch together into diagonal rows. Stitch the rows together.

Pieced Border Assembly

- Stitch together a light outer border triangle and a dark outer border triangle. Make 30 pairs.

- For the top and bottom borders, stitch together 7 pairs and add a dark outer border triangle to the end. Measure the quilt from side to side and adjust the borders to this measurement.

- For the side borders, stitch together 8 pairs and add a dark outer border triangle to the end. Measure the quilt from top to bottom and adjust the borders to this measurement.

- Stitch a side border to each side of the quilt. Stitch the top and bottom borders to the quilt. Sew an outer border corner triangle to each corner.

Final Border Assembly

- Measure the quilt from top to bottom. Trim 2 - 7 1/2" strips of the final border to this length. Measure the quilt from side to side. Trim the remaining 7 1/2" strip of the final border to this length. Stitch a side border to each side of the quilt. Sew the remaining strip to the bottom of the quilt.

Finishing

- Quilt as desired and bind.

Assembly Diagram

E (small light triangle)

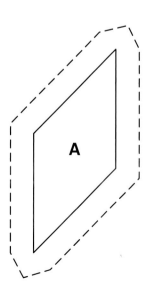

A

MIRANDA'S GARDEN

Dale Drake
Martinsville, Indiana
34" x 38"

Miranda Bostwick Stilson, born in 1817 in Delaware County, New York, made my inspiration quilt before she married James G. Fisher in 1839. She signed the back in cross stitch: "Mxxxxxx Bx Sxxxxxx No 10". While we don't know if this was her tenth quilt or merely her tenth piece of bedding, we do know that after she married she raised three children and that she died in 1886. Through good fortune, the quilt is now in my possession.

While studying this quilt, I was intrigued by the garden maze setting and the gigantic sawtooth triangle borders on three sides. I decided to replicate the quilt with half-size variable star blocks, retaining enough rows to develop the garden maze pattern. My quilt is hand pieced and hand quilted using reproduction indigo prints, and I replicated Miranda's technique of appliquéing the cross-bars on the garden maze sashing.

While Miranda's quilt is basically a simple one, I learned that she was meticulous in her attention to detail. The garden maze cross-bars, if followed from bottom to top, criss-cross each other as a lattice would – left over right, then right over left, etc. She was equally meticulous in the quilting pattern in the sashings. Each leaf motif runs from bottom to top along the vertical sashes, and from outside in along the horizontal sashes. I made sure my quilt followed the same patterns, and I think Miranda would be pleased with the result.

MIRANDA'S GARDEN

Instructions are for a quilt that measures 32" x 36"

Fabric Requirements

- 1 1/2 yards light
- 1 yard indigo print for piecing (includes binding)
- 1/2 yard indigo stripe for star block borders and lattice
  (Note: more may be needed for stripe repeats.)

Cutting Directions

From light, cut:

- 56 – 1 1/2" squares star block corners
- 14 – 3 1/4" squares, cut twice on the diagonal to make 56 triangles for star point backgrounds
- 24 – 3 3/4" squares, cut once on the diagonal to make 48 triangles to surround star block
- 8 – 2 1/2" x 7" rectangles for vertical sashing
- 3 – 2 1/2" x 24" strips for horizontal sashing
- 11 – 4 7/8" squares for half-square triangle border

From indigo print, cut:

- 14 – 2 1/2" squares for star block centers
- 56 – 1 7/8" squares, cut once on the diagonal to make 112 triangles for star points
- 11 – 4 7/8" squares for half-square triangle border

From indigo stripe, cut:

- 28 – 7/8" x 5 3/4" strips for star block borders
- 28 – 7/8" x 7" strips for star block borders
- 12 – 7/8" x 3 1/2" strips for lattice appliqué

Star Block Assembly

- Stitch a small indigo print triangle to each side of a large light triangle to make a 2 1/2" x 1 1/2" unfinished flying geese unit. Make 4 for each block.
- Stitch together the 4 flying geese units, a 2 1/2" indigo print square and 4 - 1 1/2" light squares to make a star block. Make a total of 14 star blocks that measure 4 1/2" unfinished.

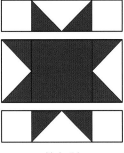

Make 14

Bordering Star Blocks

- Set aside 2 star blocks for the bottom border. Stitch a background triangle cut from a 3 3/4" square on opposite sides of a star block. Repeat with the remaining 2 sides. Center the star block and trim to 5 3/4". Stitch 2 - 5 3/4" indigo striped pieces to opposite sides of the block. Repeat on the remaining 2 sides with 7" indigo print striped pieces. The bordered star block should measure 7" unfinished. Repeat for a total of 12 bordered star blocks.

Make 12

Quilt Center Assembly

- Refer to the assembly diagram. Stitch together 4 rows, each with 3 bordered star blocks and 2 vertical sashing rectangles. Stitch a horizontal sashing strip between the rows to make the quilt center. Press under 1/4" on the long sides of the indigo striped pieces. Turn under 1/4" on the short sides of the strips as they are appliquéd to the quilt to form the lattice.

Pieced Border

- Draw a diagonal line on the wrong side of the 4 7/8" light squares. Place atop a 4 7/8" indigo print square right sides together. Sew 1/4" on either side of the line. Cut on the line and press toward the dark. Make 22 half-square triangle blocks that measure 4 1/2" unfinished.

- Refer to the assembly diagram and stitch together 2 strips of 8 half-square triangle blocks. Sew one to each side of the quilt. Measure the quilt from side to side. Stitch together 6 half-square triangle blocks and add a remaining star block to each end using a scant 1/4" seam. Adjust the seam allowances so the strip matches the side to side measurement. Stitch to the bottom of the quilt.

Assembly Diagram

Finishing

- Quilt as desired and bind.

PETITE BATIK LE MOYNE

Donna Starley
Logan, Utah
22.5" x 20.5"

"Of course I'd participate in AQSG Star Quilt Study!" With the last name of Starley, do you think I had a choice? I love stars! I have been collecting antique star quilts for a few years! One of my personal goals is to reproduce my star quilt collection in miniature. What a terrific opportunity to start that process!

This scaled down replica study quilt is a quarter the size of the original charming, yet simplistic cheddar and pink Le Moyne Star quilt, c. 1890s. While designing my study quilt, I took full advantage of a computerized quilting program to plan and draft the quilt. The 42 foundation pieced star blocks in the study quilt are exactly 2" squares, while the handcrafted blocks in the inspirational quilt vary in size (from 7" - 8" squares). I believe what I gained in precision using the computer and foundation piecing; I may have lost in charm and character. My replica quilt has over 1,436 separate units of batik fabrics in bright, sunshine yellow and over-dyed hot pink to mimic colors in the original quilt. I believe the batik fabrics added a little charm back into the quilt. I finished the study quilt with stitching in the ditch around each of the Le Moyne stars. The original inspiration quilt was machine quilted on a treadle machine with an overall straight line pattern.

It is amazing that the inspiration quilt has survived for over a century! My only hope is that both the original and mini-replica quilt will be loved, cherished and cared for another 100 years.

PETITE BATIK LE MOYNE

Instructions are for a quilt that measures 22 1/2" x 20 1/2".

This is a miniature foundation pieced quilt. There are many little pieces to sew before you can begin assembly but the results are worth it! These instructions assume you know how to paper piece. If not, refer to your favorite how-to book to learn how.

Fabric Requirements

- 1 yard light
- 1/2 yard medium
- 5/8 yard dark
- 2/3 yard for backing

Cutting Directions

- Cut 30 squares 2 1/2" x 2 1/2" from light fabric. Set aside.
- Cut 6 squares 4 1/8" x 4 1/8" from light fabric. Cut diagonally twice to make quarter-square triangles. Set aside.
- Cut 4 squares 2 3/8" x 2 3/8" from light fabric. Cut diagonally to make half-square triangles. Set aside.
- Cut 4 strips 1" wide from light fabric. Set aside.
- Cut 4 strips 1 1/2" wide from dark fabric. Set aside.

Block Assembly

- To make each block, you need to make 4 of Piece A and Piece B (see next page).
- For all the blocks, copy or trace a total of 168 Piece A and 168 Piece B foundations. (Note: the numbers on the pieces are stitching order.)
- For Piece A, begin with the dark fabric (1). Sew the medium fabric first to one side (2), open out, press and trim, and then repeat for the other side (3). Make 4.
- For Piece B, begin with the light fabric (1). Sew the medium fabric first to one side (2), open out, press and trim, and repeat for the other side (3). Make 4.
- Arrange these units to form a block. Sew together, pressing toward dark side.
- Make 42 blocks.

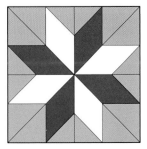

Block

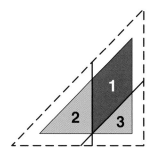

Piece A ((template, use at 100% size)

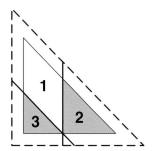

Piece B (template, use at 100% size)

Borders

To make the tiny sawtooth borders:

- Make 15 copies or trace Piece C. Each C unit has 8 Sawteeth. You need 15 units that go in one direction and 15 that go in the opposite direction. Foundation piece each unit using light and dark fabrics, pressing and trimming as you go. Be as exact as you can. Each unit of 8 Sawteeth should be 2 7/8" long finished.

- Join together 6 Sawtooth units that all go in the same direction. Join together 6 Sawtooth units that go in the other direction. These are the top and bottom borders (refer to the Assembly Diagram).

- Join together 8 Sawtooth units that all go in the same direction; remove 6 "teeth" so that the strip is 58 "teeth" long. Join together 8 Sawtooth units that go in the other direction; remove 6 "teeth" so that the strip is 58 "teeth" long. These are the side borders (see Assembly Diagram).

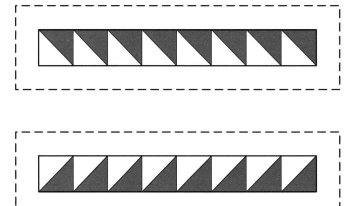

Piece C (template, use at 100% size)

Quilt Assembly

- Arrange the 30 squares, 22 quarter-square triangles, and 4 half-square triangles of light fabric with the blocks on point. Sew together. You may need to press toward the light fabric to reduce bulk.

- If you do and the dark fabrics shade through the light, trim the dark seam allowances so they will not shade.

- Sew the 2 shorter Sawtooth strips to the short edges of the top, matching centers and easing if necessary. Press. Sew the longer Sawtooth strips to the long sides of the top, matching centers and easing if necessary. Press.

- Measure the length of the top at mid-width. Cut 2 1" wide strips of light fabric to this measurement. Sew these strips to the sides of the top, matching centers and easing if necessary. Press.

- Measure the width of the top at mid-length. Cut 2 - 1" wide strips of light fabric to this measurement. Sew these strips to the top and bottom edges of the top, matching centers and easing if necessary. Press.

Finishing

- Assemble backing, batting, and top. Baste, then quilt. Bind using 1 1/2" wide strips folded over.

Assembly Diagram

GRANDMA BOWEN'S QUILT

Jonda DeLozier
Bloomington, Minnesota
26" x 26"

Stars became popular in patchwork in the late 18th century. There are more than 100 star variations and the same star can be identified by different names depending on the region of origin.

The Le Moyne Star, which has been accepted as a patchwork pattern since 1793, was named for the Le Moyne brothers who founded New Orleans in 1718. In New England it is call the Star of Le Moyne or the Lemon Star.

Patchwork consists of repeating the same geometric elements and patterns are developed through the use of color. The Le Moyne Star is created using the diamond shape.

"Applied Work" or appliqué, being used with embroidery to decorate clothing and other textiles, has been around since the Middle Ages. Conventional appliqué became popular as a primary decoration around 1840. Prior to this it was used mainly in borders. By the last half of the 19th century, a great variety of patchwork and appliqué patterns were available.

The inspiration for my quilt came after searching through several quilting and textile publications. I chose a beautiful Le Moyne Star and Cherry Wreath design created by an unknown southern Iowa quilter. Originally from Iowa, I felt a special connection to this quilt and its creator. The time and love invested in its creation is obvious. Many thanks to the unknown artist!

Grandma Bowen's Quilt

Instructions are for a quilt that measures 26" x 26".

Fabric Needed

- 1/2 yard green for vines, leaves and star points
- 1/4 yard red for star points and berries
- 1/8 yard blue for star points
- 1/2 yard binding
- 1 yard background
- 1 yard backing

Cutting

Templates are on page 96.

Wreaths

- Cut 12 blue diamonds (A).
- Cut 20 red diamonds (A).
- Cut 8 green diamonds (A).
- Cut 3/4"-wide green bias strip 108" long for wreaths (B) and stems (E).
- Cut 40 red circles (C).
- Cut 80 green leaves (D).

Border

- Cut 16 red circles (C).
- Cut 48 green leaves (D).
- Cut 128" - 3/4"-wide green bias strip for border.

Assembly

Background

- Cut a 28" x 28" background so you can trim it to size after appliqué and quilting is done. Fold it in half, then half again to find the center point. Make a mark there. Fold the background in half diagonally, then in half again. Use those lines to mark center points for the rest of wreaths, each 9" from the center.

Wreaths

Make the Le Moyne stars
- Piece together 5 Le Moyne Stars. Make 3 stars that alternate red and blue diamonds. Make 2 stars that alternate red and green diamonds. Turn under the edges.

Appliqué
- Position the pieced stars over the 5 center points marked on the background, stitch in place.
- Turn under wreath bias edges to make 1/4" wide strips, make 5. Position B wreath circle to surround the star points – use it to position the bias. Pin or baste in place.
- Next position the leaves, stems and berries as shown, underlapping the wreath. The cherries overlap the stems. Stitch in place.

Border

· Arrange the bias vine border, pin or baste in place. Arrange the leaves stems and cherries, noting that the vine overlaps them. Stitch in place.

Assembly Diagram

Finishing

· Assemble backing, batting, and top. Baste together. Quilt by machine or hand. Bind.

A

B

E

D

C

F

Add 1/4" seam allowances when cutting out these pieces.

I Can Only Imagine

Leah A. Zieber
Temecula, California
50" x 50"

I love star quilts, especially those from the early 19th century. But finding the right inspiration for my quilt was not an easy task. Nothing I saw in books or web sites fit with my ideas.

I decided that instead of just recreating a quilt which already existed, I would take elements from early star quilts and put them into my own design. I found my inspiration in a c. 1840s star quilt fragment that had only one ombre block and part of an alternate block.

I coupled the resized block with my favorite elements from early quilts such as chintz fabrics, ombre prints, blue resists, turkey reds, dress prints, toiles, serpentines, printed plaids, timeless green checks, and my favorite of all elements – the center medallion layout.

I used some of my favorite reproductions as well as a few pieces of antique fabric. Can you find them? There are three. Using a fragment as my inspiration allowed me to include those elements that I felt best represented a c. 1840s star quilt.

Since I cannot know what my inspiration quilt would have looked like; I can only imagine and create my own.

I CAN ONLY IMAGINE

Instructions are for a quilt that measures 50" x 50".

Fabric Requirements

Star Block
- 1 yard of light fabric for the backgrounds
- 1/8 yard dark fabric (can be scraps)

Medallion Block
- 1/8 yard dark fabric for center medallion star (H, L)
- 1/8 yard light fabric for center medallion star background (J, K)
- 1/8 yard dark fabric for setting triangles to put center medallion star on point (M)
- 1/4 yard stripe fabric for first mitered border (N) (depending on number of repeats, you may need more.)
- 1/4 yard light fabric for pieced border (P)
- 1/3 yard stripe fabric for second mitered border (Q) (depending on number of repeats, you may need more.)

Setting Squares and Final Border
- 3/4 yard medium fabric for setting squares (R)
- 1 1/2 yard stripe fabric for final border (S)

Cutting Directions

For each Star block
- A — Cut 1 square 2" x 2" from dark fabric.
- B — Cut 8 squares 1 1/4" x 1 1/4" from light fabric.
- C — Cut 12 rectangles 2" x 1 1/4" from light fabric.
- D — Cut 24 squares 1 1/4" x 1 1/4" from dark fabric.
- E — Cut 2 squares 2 3/4" x 2 3/4" from light fabric then cut in half diagonally.
- F — Cut 2 squares 2 1/8" x 2 1/8" from light fabric then cut in half diagonally.
- G — Cut 4 squares 1 3/8" x 1 3/8" from light fabric then cut in half diagonally.

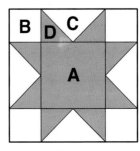

Star Block center

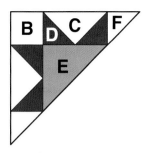

Star Block corners

Block Assembly

1. Lay dark square D on top of light rectangle C, right sides together, lining up the edges on short side of rectangle. Sew from outer corner diagonally across D through center of the long side of C; press toward center side of C.

2. Lay dark square D on top of C from step 1, right sides together on the other short end of C. Sew from outer corner diagonally across D through same center of the long side of C; press toward center side of C. You should have a Flying Geese unit now. Sew 12 of these.

3. Arrange squares B, Flying Geese units, and center square A as shown above; sew pieces and units in rows, then sew rows together.

4. Arrange squares B, Flying Geese units, triangle E, and triangles F as shown above; sew pieces and units in rows, then sew rows together. Add G Triangles to the completed square unit from step 3.

5. Arrange triangle units from step 4 and square units from step 3; sew together.

6. Repeat for 19 more blocks, for a total of 20.

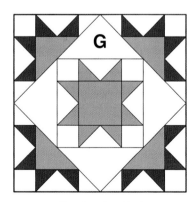

Complete Star block

Center Medallion Assembly

- H — Cut 1 square 2 5/8" x 2 5/8" from dark fabric.
- J — Cut 4 rectangles 2 5/8" x 1 7/16" from light fabric.
- K — Cut 4 squares 1 /7/16" x 1 7/16" from light fabric.
- L — Cut 8 squares 1 7/16" x 1 7/16" from dark fabric.
- Construct center medallion star as in steps 1 through 4 above.

- M — Cut 2 squares 3 7/8" x 3 7/8" from dark fabric then cut in half diagonally.
  - Sew triangles M to center medallion star, matching centers, pinning, and easing in fullness. Press toward triangles.
- N — Cut 4 rectangles 9 1/2" x 2" from stripe fabric.
  - Sew rectangles N to above star on point; miter corners. Press to outside.
- P — Cut 80 squares 1 3/8" x 1 3/8" from light fabric.
  - Sew 16 squares into one unit that is 8 squares wide x 2 squares tall; make 2 of these.
  - Sew 24 squares into one unit that is 12 squares wide x 2 squares tall; make 2 of these.
  - Sew 16-square units to 2 opposite sides of the star on point unit, matching centers, pinning, and easing in fullness. Press toward star unit.
  - Sew 24-square units to remaining opposite sides of the star on point unit, matching centers, pinning, and easing in fullness. Press toward star unit.
- Q — Cut 4 rectangles 18 1/2" x 3 1/4" from stripe fabric.
  - Sew rectangles Q to above star on point unit; miter corners. Press to outside.

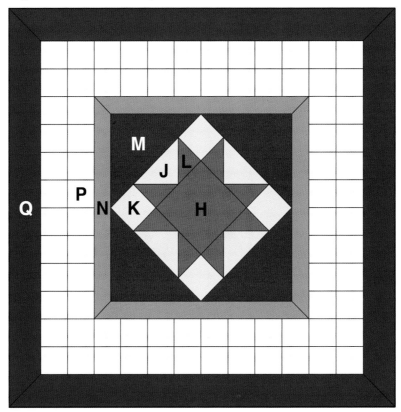

Center Medallion

Quilt Assembly

- R — Cut 20 squares 6 1/2" x 6 1/2" from medium fabric for setting squares.
  - Arrange blocks, setting squares, and center medallion.
  - Sew top 2 rows of blocks and setting squares together, pressing toward setting squares; repeat with bottom 2 rows.
  - Sew side rows together, pressing toward setting squares.

- Sew side row units to center medallion, matching centers, pinning, and easing in fullness. Press toward medallion.
- Sew top and bottom row units to center medallion and side rows, matching centers, pinning, and easing in fullness. Press toward the medallion.
- S — Cut 4 rectangles of striped fabric 50 1/2" x 4 1/2".
  - Sew rectangles to above top; miter corners. Press toward outside.

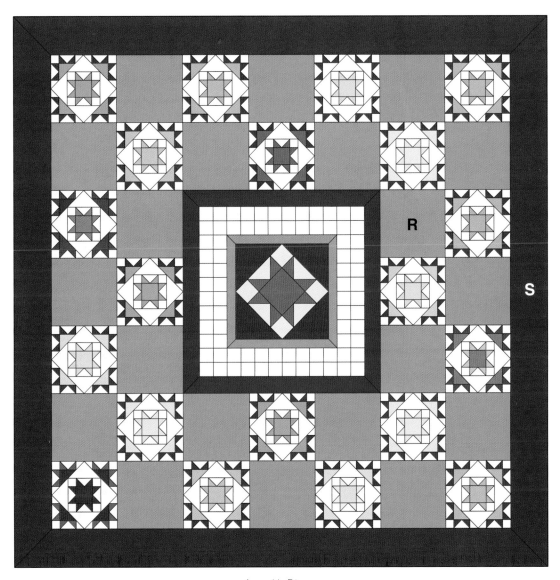

Assembly Diagram

Finishing

Assemble backing, batting, and top and baste together. Quilt by machine or hand. Turn in edges of top and back to make a knife edge and stitch closed.

TOUCHING STARS

Judith Thompson
Wenonah, New Jersey
30.5" x 30"

The bold colors of red, blue, green and stunning yellow used to create visually appealing stars was the immediate draw of this nine touching stars quilt. The condition is fresh and vibrant, indicating very little use. Perhaps this quilt was used for special occasions.

The construction of the study quilt was done using the methods of the original maker, hand piecing and hand quilting. The pieced stars in this study quilt are much smaller and just four stars are replicated. The narrow binding was made by bringing the back around to the front.

The detailed quilting has been replicated using the motifs from the original quilt. The stars have simple quilting lines following the radiation of the points. Alternate block quilting is very detailed. There are feathered wreaths with double rod quilting. There are stars in some wreaths. Random single feathers or stars fill corners of wreath blocks. The hand quilting is very fine. White thread was used for the piecing and the quilting.

The batting of the original quilt is very thin. The study quilt has very thin, almost nonexistent batting.

The challenge of studying this quilt was to find similar strong colors. The color combination was exciting. One wonders if the quilter was of Germanic descent. This typical Pennsylvania Dutch palette and a surname, Zold, are clues.

A modern quilter would be challenged to hand piece a large quilt of nine stars with 128 pieces per star. One can admire the work of a mid-19th century quilter who had basic hand sewing tools and no high intensity electric lamp.

TOUCHING STARS

Instructions are for a quilt that measures 30" x 30".

Fabric Requirements

- 1 yard light for background (includes binding)
- 3/8 yard red for star
- 1/4 yard blue print for star
- 1/4 yard yellow for star
- 1/4 yard green print for star

Cutting Directions

These instructions are for one block. Make 4 blocks total.

Template is on page 106.

From light, cut:
- 4 squares using template A
- 4 triangles using template B

From red, cut:
- 48 diamonds using template C

From blue print, cut:
- 32 diamonds using template C

From yellow, cut:
- 24 diamonds using template C

From green, cut:
- 24 diamonds using template C

Star Block Assembly

- Stitch the diamonds shapes together and make the following strips. Make 8 of each strip for one Star Block.

- Stitch together the 4 strips to make a pieced star section. Make 8.

- Stitch together 2 pieced star sections. Make 4 of these units.

- Stitch the 4 units together to form the star.
- Inset the light A squares on the corners of the block. Inset the light B triangles to complete the star block. Make 4 blocks.

Quilt Assembly

- Stitch the 4 star blocks together.

Finishing

- Quilt as desired and bind. Backing can be brought forward to make the binding, as in the original quilt.

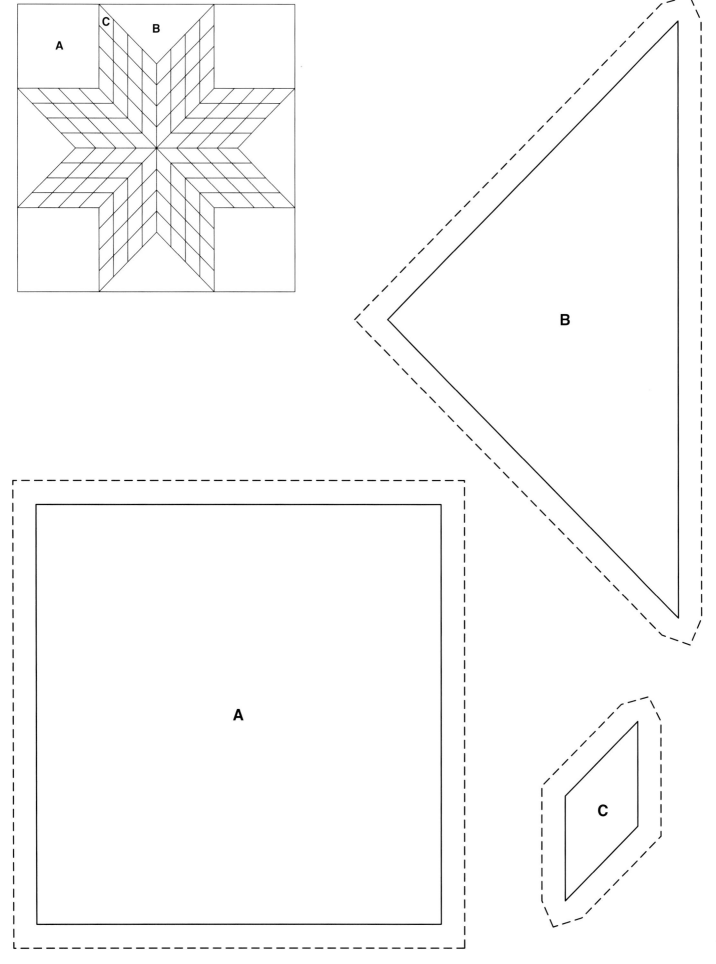

A

B

C

National Museum of American History, Smithsonian Institution

SILK STARS OF THE BLUEGRASS

Marti Phelps
Prince Frederick, Maryland
35" x 35"

I have always been fascinated with 19th century quilting from Kentucky. Being a docent at the Smithsonian, I show two exquisite Kentucky quilts on my tours. One belonged to Mary Hise Norton of Russellville, Kentucky in the second quarter of the 19th century. It was donated to the Smithsonian in 1981 by Mary's great-granddaughter, Mrs. Bonita Abernathy.

I was overjoyed when AQSG decided to celebrate 19th century star quilts. I have wanted to work with silk and this project gave me the challenge. "Blazing Stars" was totally hand-pieced and hand-quilted. I am a machine-quilter and so my quilt is machine-pieced, machine-appliquéd, and machine-quilted. I backed the silk with stabilizer before cutting it for ease of use. "Blazing Stars" had stuffed work flower and foliage motifs. I used wool batting behind digitized machine embroidery for my stuffed work.

The greatest part of this project for me, however, was locating Mrs. Abernathy and discussing the quilt with her. She is 87 years old and resides in Kevil, Kentucky.

SILK STARS OF THE BLUEGRASS

Instructions are for a quilt that measures 35" x 35"

Fabric Requirements

- For star blocks, 1/8 yard of 3 fabrics for each star
- 2 yards light green for background
- 1/3 yard for binding

Cutting Directions

These instructions are for one block. Make 25 blocks total.

Templates are on page 111.

From light green, cut:
- 4 squares using template A
- 4 triangles using template B

From first star fabric, cut:
- 12 diamonds using template C for star center and star points

From second star fabric, cut:
- 4 diamonds using template C for star center

From third star fabric, cut:
- 16 diamonds using template C for middle row of star

Star Block Assembly

- Stitch together a star point diamond to a middle row diamond. Stitch a star center diamond to a middle row diamond. Stitch the 2 units together. Make 4 units using first fabric for the star center. Make 4 units using the second fabric for the star center.

- Stitch together a unit with the first fabric for the center and a unit with the second fabric for the center. Make 4 of these units.

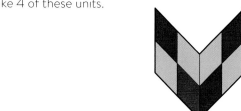

- Stitch the 4 units together to form the star.

- Inset the light green A squares on the corners of the block. Inset the light green B triangles to complete the star block. Make 25 blocks.

Quilt Assembly

- Lay out the squares in 5 rows of 5 blocks each. Stitch the blocks together into rows. Stitch the rows together.

Finishing

- Quilt as desired and bind.

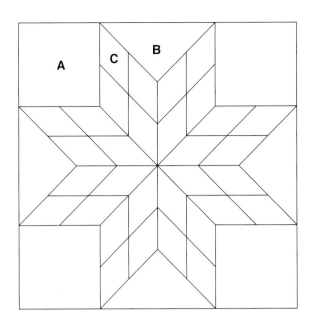

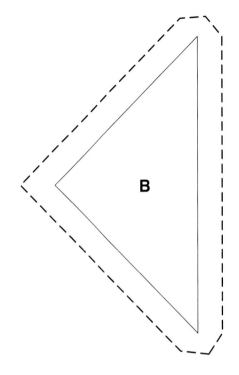

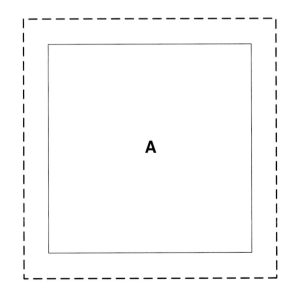

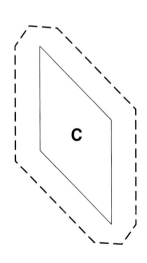

The American Quilt Study Group is believed to be the oldest and largest member organization dedicated to quilt-related studies in the world.

The American Quilt Study Group is a non-profit quilt research organization with more than 1,000 members in the U.S. and abroad. Founded in 1980 in Mill Valley, California by Sally Garoutte with a small group gathered around Sally's kitchen table, AQSG has grown into a unique and highly respected international organization.

The American Quilt Study Group sets standards for quilt studies, and provides opportunities to increase knowledge about quilts and textiles, their history and their place in society.

American Quilt Study Group members encompass all age groups and include quilters and non-quilters alike. Membership is comprised of traditional and contemporary quilt artists, quilt lovers, historians, researchers, collectors, dealers, folklorists, authors, museum curators, quilt appraisers, and students of women's studies.

If you are interested in quilts and quilting, their history and role in society; and you would like to help promote and preserve this traditional yet ever-changing art, join us!

Members of AQSG participate in the effort to preserve quilt heritage through our various publications, extensive research opportunities, yearly Seminar and membership contacts.

Your membership includes *Blanket Statements*, a quarterly newsletter; *Uncoverings*, an annual journal of the papers presented at our Seminar; research information; the opportunity to join our Yahoo Groups chat list and the opportunity to attend our yearly Seminar.

Levels of Membership Support

- $65 Friend
- $55 Senior (65+)
- $55 Student (full-time)
- $110 Associate
- $110 Corporation/Organization

Canada please add $5.50 for postage; all other countries please add $19 for postage.

American Quilt Study Group
1610 L Street
Lincoln, NE 68508

http://www.americanquiltstudygroup.org
Become a fan of American Quilt Study Group on Facebook.

facebook